Agatha Christie

Agatha Christie (1890-1976) is known throughout the world as the Queen of Crime. Her books have sold over a billion copies in English with another billion in over 100 foreign languages. She is the most widely published and translated author of all time and in any language; only the Bible and Shakespeare have sold more copies. She is the author of 80 crime novels and short story collections, 19 plays, and six other novels. *The Mousetrap*, her most famous play, was first staged in 1952 in London and is still performed there – it is the longest-running play in history.

Agatha Christie's first novel was published in 1920. It featured Hercule Poirot, the Belgian detective who has become the most popular detective in crime fiction since Sherlock Holmes. Collins has published Agatha Christie since 1926.

This series has been especially created for readers worldwide whose first language is not English. Each story has been shortened, and the vocabulary and grammar simplified to make it accessible to readers with a good intermediate knowledge of the language.

The following features are included after the story:

A **List of characters** to help the reader identify who is who, and how they are connected to each other. **Cultural notes** to explain historical and other references. A **Glossary** of words that some readers may not be familiar with are explained. There is also a **Recording** of the story.

Agatha Christie

N or M?

Collins

Collins

HarperCollins Publishers
77–85 Fulham Palace Road
Hammersmith, London W6 8JB
www.collinselt.com

Collins ® is a registered trademark of HarperCollins Publishers Limited.

This *Collins English Readers Edition* published 2012

Reprint 10 9 8 7 6 5 4 3 2 1 0

Original text first published in Great Britain by Collins 1941

AGATHA CHRISTIE™ N or M?™ Copyright © 1941 Agatha Christie Limited. All rights reserved. Copyright © 2012 N or M?™ abridged edition Agatha Christie Limited. All rights reserved.
www.agathachristie.com

ISBN: 978-85-7827-517-4

A catalogue record for this book is available from the British Library.

Educational Consultant: Fitch O'Connell

Cover by crushed.co.uk © HarperCollins/Agatha Christie Ltd 2008

Typeset by Aptara in India

Printed and bound in Great Britain by Clays Ltd, St Ives plc

All rights reserved. No part of this publication may be reproduced, stored in a retrieval system, or transmitted, in any form or by any means, electronic, mechanical, photocopying, recording or otherwise, without the prior permission of the publishers.

This book is sold subject to the condition that it shall not, by way of trade or otherwise, be lent, re-sold, hired out or otherwise circulated without the publisher's prior consent in any form of binding or cover other than that in which it is published and without a similar condition including this condition being imposed on the subsequent purchaser.

HarperCollins does not warrant that www.collinselt.com or any other website mentioned in this title will be provided uninterrupted, that any website will be error free, that defects will be corrected, or that the website or the server that makes it available are free of viruses or bugs. For full terms and conditions please refer to the site terms provided on the website.

Contents

Story   1

Character list   94

Cultural notes   96

Glossary   101

Chapter 1

It was the spring of 1940. Tommy Beresford made sure he was smiling as he walked into the sitting-room where his wife sat knitting. Mrs Beresford looked up at him. 'Anything interesting in the evening newspaper?'

'Things look bad in France,' Tommy said. 'Well, why don't you ask me how it went?'

'Darling, I don't need to ask,' said Tuppence. 'You are smiling the unhappiest smile I have ever seen.'

'As bad as that?'

'Much worse!'

'I tell you, Tuppence, it's terrible when a man of forty-six is made to feel like a grandfather. Army, Navy, Air Force, Foreign Office, they all say the same – I'm too old. They don't want me in any job.'

'It's the same for me,' complained Tuppence. 'They don't want people of my age for nursing. They'd rather have a schoolgirl who's never seen a wound than a woman who worked in the Great War.'

'Well, it is comforting that Deborah has a job,' Tommy said.

'I could do as much as our daughter,' remarked Tuppence.

Tommy grinned. '*She* wouldn't think so.'

Tuppence gave a cry of anger. 'Are we too old to do things? Isn't it true that we once caught a dangerous criminal? Isn't it true that we rescued a girl and important secret documents, and were thanked by a grateful country? Us! That was us! I'm *so* disappointed in Mr Carter.'

'But he no longer works in Intelligence. He's old. He lives in Scotland and fishes.'

Tuppence sighed sadly. 'I wish we could find a job – any job. I imagine the worst when I have so much time to think.' As she spoke she looked at the photograph of a very young man in an Air Force uniform, with the same wide smile as his father Tommy's.

The doorbell rang. Tuppence got up. She opened the door to see a broad-shouldered man with a large, fair moustache and a cheerful red face.

'Are you Mrs Beresford? My name is Grant. I'm a friend of Lord Easthampton's. He suggested that I visit you and your husband.'

'Oh, come in.'

She led him into the sitting room. 'Tommy, Mr Grant is a friend of Mr Car . . . of Lord Easthampton's.'

Lord Easthampton was the proper title of their old friend. But Tuppence always thought of him as *Mr Carter* – the name he used when he was Chief of Intelligence and their boss.

For a few minutes the three talked together, then Tuppence left the room. She returned a few minutes later with sherry and some glasses. Then Mr Grant said to Tommy, 'I understand you're looking for a job? Well, active service is only for the young men, but I can offer you some office work, which is better than nothing. Come to my office one day this week and . . .'

The telephone rang and Tuppence picked it up. 'Hello – yes – what?'

A loud voice, obviously in pain, spoke from the other end.

'Oh, my dear, of course, I'll come now . . .' She put down the phone. 'Tommy, that was Maureen. I'm so sorry, Mr Grant, but I must go. My friend has fallen and hurt her ankle and I must go and help her. Do forgive me.'

'Of course, Mrs Beresford.'

Tuppence hurried out. The door of the flat shut noisily.

Tommy poured another glass of sherry for his guest.

'Thank you. In one way, your wife leaving is fortunate for us. It will save time. You see, Beresford, if you had come to the Ministry, I would have asked you to do something special. Easthampton told us you were the man for the job.'

Tommy was <u>delighted</u>. 'Tell me.'

'This is <u>confidential</u>. Not even your wife must know. Officially you will be working in Scotland, in a secret army area where your wife cannot join you. In fact you will be somewhere very different. You've read in the newspapers of the <u>Fifth Column</u>? You know what that means?'

'The enemy within,' Tommy said.

'Exactly. You know the war started badly for us. We did not want war and had not prepared for it. Well, we are correcting our mistakes and we can win this war – but only if we do not lose it first. And the danger of losing it comes, not from Germany, but from within. The Fifth Column is here, men and women in positions of power who believe in Nazi aims and want a Nazi government here.

'And we don't know who they are. We know there are at least two in powerful positions in the Navy, one in the army and three in the Air Force – and several members in Intelligence. We know because secret information is being given to the enemy.'

'But what can I do? I don't know any of these people.'

Grant nodded. 'Exactly. And they don't know you. But these people do know our agents, so I cannot use them. That is why I went to Easthampton and he thought of you. It's twenty years since you worked for the department. Your face and name are not known. What do you say? Will you take the job?'

Tommy could not stop smiling. 'I certainly will!'

'Well, Beresford, you'll take the place of the best man we had, Farquhar. He was hit by a lorry – and that was not an accident. All he managed to say before he died was, "N or M. Song Susie."'

'That doesn't seem helpful!'

Grant smiled. 'N and M are two of the most important German agents. N, we know, is a man. M is a woman, and they are in England.'

'I see. And Farquhar?'

'Farquhar must have been <u>on their trail</u>. Song Susie sounds very strange – but Farquhar spoke French badly. There was a train ticket in his pocket, to Leahampton, a town on the south coast. Lots of hotels and guesthouses. There is one called *Sans Souci*, which means, of course, "without worries" in French – a good name for a guesthouse!'

Tommy said, 'Song Susie – *Sans Souci*. I see. And your idea is that I go there and see what I can find.'

'Exactly.'

Tommy smiled again.

★ ★ ★

Tommy went to Scotland three days later. Tuppence said goodbye at the station, her eyes bright with tears. Once there, he took a train back to England again the next day. On the third day he arrived at Leahampton.

Sans Souci was built on the side of a hill and had a good view of the sea from its upper windows. The owner, Mrs Perenna, was a middle-aged woman with a lot of black hair and a smile that showed a lot of very white teeth.

Tommy mentioned that his cousin, Miss Meadowes, had stayed at *Sans Souci* two years ago. Mrs Perenna remembered Miss Meadowes. 'Such a dear old lady.'

Tommy agreed. There was, he knew, a real Miss Meadowes – the department was careful about these details.

'And how is dear Miss Meadowes?'

Tommy explained sadly that Miss Meadowes had died. Mrs Perenna said the proper words with the correct sadness. But she was soon talking happily again. She had a room for Mr Meadowes with a lovely sea view. She thought Mr Meadowes was right to leave London. Very unpleasant these days.

Still talking, Mrs Perenna took Tommy upstairs and showed him the bedroom. He found himself wondering what her nationality was. The name was Spanish or Portuguese, but that could be her husband's nationality. She might, he thought, be Irish.

It was agreed that Mr Meadowes should move in the following day. Tommy arrived at six o'clock. Mrs Perenna came out to welcome him, gave instructions about his luggage to a maid, and then led him into the lounge.

'I always introduce my guests,' said Mrs Perenna, smiling at the five people there, who looked at him suspiciously. 'This is our new arrival, Mr Meadowes – Mrs O'Rourke.'

A very large woman with a moustache gave him a bright smile.

'<u>Major</u> Bletchley.'

Major Bletchley, obviously retired a long time ago from the army, nodded.

'Mr von Deinim.'

A young man, very stiff, fair-haired and blue-eyed, got up and <u>bowed</u>.

'Miss Minton.'

An elderly woman, wearing many necklaces, was knitting a <u>balaclava</u>. She smiled and laughed.

'And Mrs Blenkensop.'

More knitting. A dark-haired woman lifted her eyes from another balaclava. Her eyes met his – polite, uninterested stranger's eyes. The room seemed to spin round him. Tuppence! Mrs Blenkensop was Tuppence!

Chapter 2

At dinner four more guests of *Sans Souci* appeared – a middle-aged couple, Mr and Mrs Cayley, and a young mother, Mrs Sprot, who had come with her baby girl from London. She was placed next to Tommy and asked, 'Do you think it's safe now in London? Everyone seems to be going back.'

Before Tommy could reply, Miss Minton spoke up, 'You must not risk going back. Think of your sweet little Betty. You know they say that the <u>Blitzkrieg</u> on England is coming soon – and a new type of poisonous gas, I believe.'

After dinner everyone moved into the lounge. The women started knitting again and Tommy had to listen to an extremely boring account of Major Bletchley's experiences in India.

The fair young man went out, bowing at the door. Major Bletchley interrupted his own story to say to Tommy, 'He's a <u>refugee</u>. Got out of Germany a month before the war.'

'He's a German?'

'Yes. His father was in trouble for criticizing the Nazis. Two of his brothers are in <u>concentration camps</u>.'

The following morning Tommy rose early and walked down to the sea front. He saw a familiar figure coming in the other direction. Tommy raised his hat. 'Good morning,' he said pleasantly. 'Mrs Blenkensop, is it not? How did you get here? Tell me how you managed it, Tuppence.'

'The moment Grant talked of our Mr Carter I knew it wouldn't be an office job – and that I was not going to be allowed to join in. So when I went to get the sherry, I ran downstairs to the Browns' apartment and telephoned Maureen. I told her to call me and what to say. She rang. I rushed off. Banged the hall door, but stayed inside, and then I simply listened to Mr Grant.'

'And you <u>overheard</u> everything?'

'Everything,' smiled Tuppence happily.

'But why call yourself Blenkensop?' Tommy asked.

'Why not? Why did you choose Meadowes?'

'I didn't choose it. I was told to name myself Meadowes. Mr Meadowes has a respectable past, which I have learnt.'

'Very nice,' said Tuppence. 'Are you married?'

'My wife died ten years ago in Singapore.'

'Why in Singapore?'

'We've all got to die somewhere. What's wrong with Singapore?'

'Oh, nothing. It's probably a most suitable place to die. I'm a <u>widow</u>. Not very intelligent and I sometimes say silly things.'

'Where did your husband die?'

'Probably at home. I suppose he died of too much alcohol. I have three sons: Douglas, who is in the Navy; Raymond is in the Air Force and Cyril, my youngest son, is in the Army. Now, how are we going to cooperate?'

Tommy said thoughtfully, 'We mustn't be seen too much together.'

'No. I think <u>chasing</u> is best.'

'Chasing?'

'I chase you. I've had two husbands and I'm looking for a third. You are the hunted <u>widower</u>. Every now and then I catch you. Everyone laughs and thinks it very funny.'

'Sounds perfect,' agreed Tommy. He caught her arm. 'Look over there.'

Near the <u>pier</u> they saw Carl von Deinim listening to a girl who was talking forcefully.

'I think this is where you leave me,' Tuppence <u>murmured</u>.

'Right,' agreed Tommy. He turned and walked off in the opposite direction.

Tuppence slowly continued her walk. As she passed the young couple she overheard a few words.

'But you must be careful, Carl. The least suspicion . . .'

Words that suggested something? Yes, but they could mean anything. She turned and again passed the two. More words from the girl floated to her.

'Arrogant English, how I hate them!'

Mrs Blenkensop's eyebrows rose. Carl von Deinim was a refugee from the Nazis, living in safety in England. It was not wise of him to listen to such words. Again Tuppence turned. But this time the couple had parted, the girl to cross the road, Carl von Deinim to wait for Tuppence. He quickly bowed.

Tuppence gave a silly laugh, 'Good morning, Mr von Deinim, isn't it? Such a lovely morning.'

'Ah, yes. The weather is fine.'

'Yes, it is,' Tuppence said. 'I don't often come out before breakfast. And this little walk has given me quite an appetite.'

'You go back to *Sans Souci* now? If you permit, I will walk with you.'

'Are you also out to get an appetite?' inquired Tuppence.

He shook his head. 'Oh no. My breakfast, I have already had it. I am on my way to work.'

'Work?'

'I am a research chemist. I came to this country to escape Nazi persecution. I had very little money – no friends. I do now what useful work I can.'

He stared straight ahead. Tuppence was conscious of the strong emotions he was trying to hide.

She answered vaguely, 'Oh, yes, I see.'

'My two brothers are in concentration camps. My father died in one. My mother died of sadness and fear.'

Tuppence thought, 'The way he says that – it's as if he had memorised it.'

They walked in silence for some moments. Two men passed them. Tuppence heard one say to his companion, 'I'm sure that man is a German.'

Carl von Deinim's hidden emotions came to the surface. 'You heard – you heard – that is what they say – I . . .'

'My dear boy', Tuppence suddenly returned to being her real self, 'don't be an idiot. You can't have it both ways. You're alive, that's the main thing. Alive and free. But this country's at war and you're a German.' She smiled suddenly. 'You can't expect the man in the street to know whether you're a bad German or a good German.'

He stared at her. Then suddenly he too smiled. 'To be a good German I must be on time at my work. Good morning.'

Tuppence stared after him then she said to herself, 'Mrs Blenkensop, you stopped being a silly man-chaser then. Pay more attention in future. Now for breakfast.'

★ ★ ★

Inside *Sans Souci* Mrs Perenna was having a conversation with someone.

'And get the cooked ham at Quillers – it was cheaper last time there, and be careful about the vegetables . . .' She stopped as Tuppence entered.

'Oh, good morning, Mrs Blenkensop, you're up early. Breakfast is all ready in the dining-room.' She pointed to her companion, 'This is my daughter, Sheila. You haven't met her. She only came home last night.'

Tuppence looked with interest at Sheila – the girl she had just seen talking to Carl von Deinim. Tuppence said a few pleasant words and went into the dining-room. There were three people having breakfast – Mrs Sprot and her baby girl, and Mrs O'Rourke.

The old woman looked at Tuppence with huge interest. 'It's a fine thing to be out walking before breakfast,' she remarked. 'A grand appetite it gives you.'

'Nice bread and milk, darling,' said Mrs Sprot to her daughter, trying to put a spoonful into the child's mouth, but baby Betty cleverly avoided this by a quick movement of her head and stared at Tuppence with large round eyes. She pointed a milky finger at the newcomer, gave her a brilliant smile and said, 'Gaga bouch.'

'She likes you,' cried Mrs Sprot, smiling warmly at Tuppence.

'Bouch,' said Betty Sprot. 'Ah pooth ah bag,' she added.

'And what does she mean by that?' demanded Mrs O'Rourke with interest.

'She doesn't speak very clearly yet,' <u>confessed</u> Mrs Sprot. 'She's only just over two, you know. She can say "Mama", though, can't you, darling?'

Betty looked thoughtfully at her mother and said, 'Cuggle bick.'

'It's a language of their own they have, the little angels,' said Mrs O'Rourke. 'Betty, darling, say "Mama" now.'

Betty looked hard at Mrs O'Rourke, <u>frowned</u> and said with great emphasis, 'Nazer.'

'She's doing her best! And a lovely sweet girl she is.' Mrs O'Rourke stood up with difficulty, smiled in a frightening manner at Betty, and walked slowly out of the room.

'Ga, ga, ga,' said Betty with huge satisfaction, and beat the table with her spoon.

Tuppence asked with a grin, 'What does Nazer really mean?'

'I'm afraid it's what Betty says when she doesn't like anyone or anything.' Mrs Sprot said, her face reddening.

'I thought so', said Tuppence laughing.

'Mrs O'Rourke tries to be kind,' said Mrs Sprot, 'but she is alarming with that deep voice.'

The door opened and Major Bletchley and Tommy appeared. Tuppence began to play the part of a man-chasing widow. 'Ah, Mr Meadowes,' she called out. 'I got back before you! But I've left you a little breakfast!' She pointed to the chair beside her. Tommy sat down at the other end of the table. Betty Sprot said 'Putch!' to Major Bletchley, who was delighted.

'And how's little Miss Betty this morning?'

Tuppence who was watching all of them thought, 'There must be some mistake. There can't be anything suspicious going on here. There simply can't!'

Chapter 3

On the sunny terrace outside, Miss Minton was knitting.

'Good morning, Mrs Blenkensop. I do hope you slept well.'

Mrs Blenkensop admitted that she never slept very well the first night or two in a strange bed then added, 'What a very pretty pattern that is you are knitting!'

Miss Minton looked pleased.

'I'm not very good at knitting,' Tuppence went on. 'I can only do simple things like balaclavas for the soldiers, and even now I'm afraid I've gone wrong somewhere. I'd never done any before this terrible war. But one feels that one must do something.'

'Oh yes, indeed. And you have a boy in the Navy?'

'Yes, my eldest. Then I have a boy in the Air Force and Cyril, my youngest, is out in France.'

'Oh dear, dear, how terribly worried you must be!'

Tuppence thought of her son. 'Oh Derek, my darling Derek . . . Out there in terrible danger and here I am acting the part of a worried mother — when it's what I really am!' She said aloud, 'We must all be brave, mustn't we? I was told the other day by someone in a very high position that the Germans can't possibly fight for more than another two months.'

Mr and Mrs Cayley had come out on the terrace. Mr Cayley sat in a chair and his wife put a <u>blanket</u> over his knees.

'What's that you are saying?' he asked.

'We are saying,' said Miss Minton, 'that it will all be over by the autumn.'

'Nonsense,' said Mr Cayley. 'This war is going to last at least six years.'

'Oh, Mr Cayley,' protested Tuppence. 'You don't really think so?'

'Yes,' he said. 'I give it six years. You dear ladies are being completely unrealistic. Now I know Germany very well from my business dealings before I retired. I can assure you that Germany can continue practically indefinitely with Russia behind her . . .' Mr Cayley went on, approval in his voice.

Mrs Sprot came out with Betty and sat her down with a small <u>woollen</u> dog with only one ear and a woollen doll's jacket. 'There, Betty,' she said. 'You dress up Bonzo ready for his walk while Mummy gets ready to go out.'

Betty started talking to Bonzo in her own language. 'Truckle – truckly – pah bat,' said Betty.

Mr Cayley, noticing that no one was paying him any attention, continued angrily, 'As I was saying, Germany has such a perfect system of . . .'

Tuppence could feel someone behind her. She turned her head. It was Mrs Perenna, her eyes on the group. And there was something in those eyes – <u>contempt</u>?

Tuppence thought, 'I must find out more about Mrs Perenna.'

* * *

Tommy was making friends with Major Bletchley.

'You brought some golf clubs with you, didn't you, Meadowes? We must have a game together. The course has lovely views over the sea. And it's never very crowded. What about coming along with me this morning?'

'Thanks very much. I'd like it.'

'I must say, I'm glad you've arrived,' remarked Bletchley as they were walking up the hill. 'There are too many women in that place. It gets annoying. I'm glad there's another man to talk to. You can't count Cayley – the man talks of nothing but his health. If he went out for a good ten-mile walk every day, he'd be a different man. And I'm not sure about von Deinim.'

'No?' said Tommy.

'No. This refugee business is dangerous. I'd <u>intern</u> the lot of them. We need to be cautious. Carl von Deinim came over here only a month before the war began. That's a bit suspicious.'

'Then you think . . .?' began Tommy.

'<u>Spying</u>!'

'But surely there's nothing of great military or naval importance around here?'

'But it's on the coast, isn't it? And anyone could come over here and talk about their brothers in concentration camps. He's a Nazi – that's what he is – a Nazi.'

The Major won their game of golf, which delighted him. 'Good match, Meadowes, very good match. Come along and I'll introduce you to some of the others in the clubhouse. Nice lot. Ah, here's Haydock – you'll like Haydock. Retired naval man. He has that house on the <u>cliff</u> next door to us. He's our local <u>Air Raid</u> Precaution <u>Warden</u> – you know, he <u>patrols</u> the streets at night to make sure no lights are showing to attract the German bomber pilots.'

<u>Commander</u> Haydock was a big man with intensely blue eyes and a habit of shouting most of the time.

'So you're going to keep Bletchley company at *Sans Souci*? He'll be glad of another man. Rather too many females, eh, Bletchley?'

'I'm not that much of a ladies' man,' said Major Bletchley.

'Nonsense,' said Haydock. 'Not your type of lady, my boy, that's all. Old ladies with nothing to do but talk about other people and knit.'

'You're forgetting the <u>landlady</u>'s daughter, Miss Perenna,' said Bletchley.

'Ah, Sheila. She's an attractive girl all right.'

'I'm a bit worried about her,' said Bletchley. 'She's seeing too much of that German <u>fellow</u>.'

'Hmm, that's bad. He's a good-looking young man, but we can't have that sort of thing. Making friends with the enemy – we can't allow that. There are plenty of decent young English fellows about.'

Bletchley added, 'Sheila's a strange girl – there are times when she will hardly speak to anyone.'

'Spanish blood,' said Commander Haydock. 'Her father was half Spanish, wasn't he?' He looked at his watch. 'It's time for the news. We'd better go in and listen to it.'

There was little news that day. After commenting with approval on the latest activities of the Air Force, the Commander talked about his favourite theory – that the Germans would try to land at Leahampton simply because it was such an unimportant spot. 'There's not even an anti-aircraft gun in the place! Terrible!' Haydock then gave Tommy an invitation to come and see his house, _Smugglers' Rest_. 'I've got a marvellous view – my own beach. Bring him along, Bletchley.'

It was decided that Tommy and Major Bletchley should come for drinks on the evening of the following day.

★ ★ ★

After lunch at *Sans Souci*, Mr Meadowes walked down to the pier. There were some children running up and down screaming in voices that matched the screaming of the seabirds, and one man sitting on the end, fishing. Mr Meadowes stood beside him and looked down into the water. Then he asked gently, 'Caught anything?'

The fisherman shook his head. 'I don't often catch anything,' Mr Grant said, without turning his head. 'What about you, Meadowes?'

'I've nothing much to report as yet, sir. I've made friends with Major Bletchley who seems the usual type of retired officer. Cayley seems to be a genuine invalid. However, he was in Germany frequently during the last few years. And of course there's von Deinim.'

'Yes, I'm interested in von Deinim. N or M may not be at *Sans Souci*, it may be Carl von Deinim who is there, reporting to them. Through him we may be led to them. But I can tell you in confidence, Beresford, that very nearly all Germans in this country are going to be interned.'

'You've had the other guests at *Sans Souci* checked, I suppose, sir?'

Grant sighed. 'No. I could ask the department to check easily enough but I can't risk it, Beresford. I'm not sure we don't have a traitor in the department itself. If anyone guesses that I'm watching *Sans Souci*, then the organization may find out. That's why you've got to work without help from us. They must not know. There's only one person I've been able to check up on.'

'Who's that, sir?'

'Carl von Deinim. That was easy enough because it's routine to check foreigners.'

'And what was the result?'

'Carl is exactly what he says he is. His father, who was against the Nazis, was arrested and died in a concentration camp. Carl's elder brothers are in camps. His mother died a year ago. He got to England a month before war began. Von Deinim said he wanted to help this country and his work in a chemical research laboratory has been excellent.'

'Then he's all right?'

'Not necessarily. There are two possibilities. The whole von Deinim family could be deceiving us. Or else this is not the real Carl von Deinim but a man playing the part of Carl von Deinim.'

'He seems a very nice young man,' said Tommy slowly.

Sighing unhappily Grant replied, 'They nearly always are. But what about the women in this place?'

'I think there's something strange about the woman who runs it.'

'Mrs Perenna?'

'Yes. There's a young mother; an unmarried woman who knits; the invalid's stupid wife; and a rather terrifying-looking old Irishwoman. All seem harmless enough.'

'That's everyone?'

'No. There's a Mrs Blenkensop – arrived three days ago.'

'Well?' demanded Grant.

'Mrs Blenkensop is my wife.'

'What? I thought I told you not to say a word to your wife!'

'And I didn't.' With a quiet pride, Tommy told Grant what Tuppence had done. There was a silence. Then Grant laughed.

'She's wonderful! Easthampton told me not to leave her out. I wouldn't listen to him. It shows you, though, how careful you've got to be not to be overheard. Yes, she's a smart woman, your wife. Tell her the department will consider it an honour if she will agree to work with us.'

'I'll tell her,' said Tommy with a grin.

'I don't suppose you could persuade your wife to keep out of danger?'

Tommy said slowly, 'I wouldn't want to do that . . . Tuppence and I, you see, we go into things together, always!'

Chapter 4

When Tuppence entered the lounge at *Sans Souci* just before dinner, the only person in the room was Mrs O'Rourke, who was sitting by the window like a gigantic Buddha.

'Ah now, sit here now, Mrs Blenkensop, and tell me what you've been doing with yourself this fine day and how you like Leahampton.'

There was something about Mrs O'Rourke that fascinated Tuppence. She was like a character from a fairy tale, huge and ugly, with a deep voice like a man's. Tuppence replied that she thought she was going to like Leahampton very much, and be happy there.

'That is,' she added in an unhappy voice, 'as happy as I can be anywhere with this terrible <u>anxiety</u> that's with me all the time.'

'Ah now, don't you be worrying yourself. Those boys of yours will come back to you <u>safe and sound</u>. One of them's in the Air Force, I think you said?'

'Yes, Raymond.'

'And is he in France now, or in England?'

'He's in Egypt according to his last letter – well, that's not exactly what he *said* – we have a little private <u>code</u>, if you know what I mean? You see I feel I must know just where he is.'

Mrs O'Rourke nodded her Buddha-like head. 'I know how you feel. If I had a boy out there, I'd be fooling the <u>censor</u> in the same way.'

'I feel so lost without my three boys,' Tuppence said sadly. 'There's always been at least one of them at home. So I thought I'd come somewhere quiet.'

Again the Buddha nodded. 'I agree with you entirely. London is no place to be at the present. I've lived there myself for many years now. I used to sell antiques and I had a shop in Chelsea. I had lovely stuff there and some good customers. But there you are, when there's a war on, no one is interested in buying antiques. But I'm not one of those that's always complaining – not like Mr Cayley with his illnesses and his talk of his failing business. Of course it's going badly – there's a war on – and there's his wife who never says no to him. Then there's that little Mrs Sprot, always worrying about her husband, Arthur.'

'Is he out at the <u>Front</u>?'

'No! He's a clerk in an office, and so terrified of air raids he sent his wife down here at the beginning of the war. Mind you, I think that's the best thing for the child – and a nice little girl she is – but Mrs Sprot keeps saying Arthur must miss her so. But if you ask me, Arthur's not missing *her* much!'

Tuppence murmured, 'I'm terribly sorry for all these mothers. I do understand why they are sending away the children from the cities – the Germans won't bomb the countryside, will they? But if you let your children go away without you, you never stop worrying. And if you go with them, it's hard on the husbands left at home.'

'Ah! Yes, and it becomes expensive running two homes.'

'This place seems quite a reasonable price,' said Tuppence.

'Yes, I'd say you get good value. Mrs Perenna's a strange woman though. There's been a great drama in that woman's life, I'm certain of that.'

'Do you really think so?'

'I do. And the mystery she makes of herself! "And where do you come from in Ireland?" I asked her. And would you believe it, she said she was not from Ireland at all.'

'You think she is Irish?'

'Of course she's Irish. I know my own countrywomen. I could name you the county she comes from. But there! "I'm English", she says, "and my husband was a Spaniard".' Mrs O'Rourke stopped speaking as Mrs Sprot came in, followed by Tommy.

Tuppence immediately took on a playful manner.

'Good evening, Mr Meadowes. You look very well this evening.'

'Plenty of exercise, that's the secret,' Tommy replied.

Then the rest of the party came in and the conversation during the meal was about spies. Only Sheila Perenna took no part in the conversation. She sat there, her dark face angry. Carl von Deinim was out, so everyone was speaking freely. Sheila only spoke once. Mrs Sprot said in her thin voice, 'The biggest mistake I think the Germans made in the last war was to shoot Nurse Cavell. It turned everybody against them.'

It was then that Sheila demanded, 'Why shouldn't they shoot her? She was an English spy, wasn't she? She helped English people to escape in an enemy country. Why shouldn't she be shot?'

'Oh, but shooting a woman – and a nurse.'

Sheila got up. 'I think the Germans were quite right,' she muttered. She went out of the glass door into the garden.

Everyone then went into the lounge for coffee. Only Tommy went out to the garden. He found Sheila Perenna standing by the garden wall, staring out at the sea. He offered her a cigarette, which she accepted.

'Lovely night,' he commented.

In a low voice, the girl answered, 'It could be . . .'

'If it weren't for the war, you mean?' he asked quietly.

'I don't mean that at all. I hate the war.'

'So do we all.'

'Not in the way *I* mean. I hate the horrible, horrible patriotism.'

'Patriotism?' Tommy was surprised.

'Yes, I hate patriotism! Betraying your country – dying for your country – serving your country. Why should one's country mean anything at all?'

Tommy said simply, 'I don't know. It just does.'

'Not to me! Oh, it would to you. You believe in the British Empire – and – and – the stupidity of dying for one's country.'

'My country,' said Tommy, 'won't *let* me die for it.'

'Yes, but you want to. And it's so stupid! Nothing's worth dying for. It's all an idea – talk, talk. My country doesn't mean anything to me at all.'

'Some day,' said Tommy, 'you'll find that it does.'

'No. Never. I've suffered. I've seen . . . Do you know who my father was? His name was Patrick Maguire. He – he was a follower of Casement in the last war. He was shot as a traitor! All for nothing! Why couldn't he just stay at home quietly? He's a martyr to some people and a traitor to others. I think he was just . . . stupid!'

'So that's the secret you've grown up with?'

'Yes. Mother changed her name. We lived in Spain for some years. She always says that my father was half Spanish. We always tell lies wherever we go. We've been all over Europe. Finally we came here, and I think running this guest house is the worst thing we've done yet. I hate it!'

'How does your mother feel about – things?' Tommy asked.

'You mean about my father's death?' Sheila was silent a moment, thinking carefully about the question. She said slowly, 'I've never really known . . . she never talks about it. It's not easy to know what Mother feels or thinks.'

Tommy nodded his head thoughtfully.

'I – I don't know why I've been telling you this.' Sheila said abruptly. 'I got angry. Where did it all start?'

'A discussion on Edith Cavell.'

'Oh, yes – patriotism. I said I hated it.'

'Aren't you forgetting Nurse Cavell's own words?'

'What words?'

'Before she died. Don't you know what she said?' He repeated the words, 'Patriotism is not enough . . . I must have no <u>hatred</u> in my heart.'

'Oh.' She stood there for a moment. Then, turning quickly, she ran off into the shadow of the garden.

★ ★ ★

Mrs Blenkensop stopped at the post office. She bought stamps and went into one of the public phone boxes. There she rang up a certain number and asked for Mr Faraday. This was how they contacted Mr Grant. She came out smiling and walked home, stopping on the way to buy some knitting wool.

It was a pleasant afternoon with a light wind. Tuppence changed her normally energetic walk into a slow and easy one, more like the way someone like Mrs Blenkensop would walk. Mrs Blenkensop had nothing else to do except knit and write letters to her boys. She was always writing letters to her boys – and sometimes she left them lying around, half finished.

Tuppence came slowly up the hill towards *Sans Souci*. Since the road ended at *Smugglers' Rest*, Commander Haydock's house, few people walked there. She noticed a woman standing by the gate looking inside. It was not until Tuppence was close behind her that the woman heard her and turned. She was a tall woman, poorly dressed. She was not young – probably just under forty –

blonde-haired and beautiful. Just for a minute Tuppence had a feeling that the woman was familiar. A look of fear crossed the woman's face.

'Are you looking for someone?' Tuppence said.

The woman spoke slowly, with a foreign accent. 'This house is *Sans Souci*? Can you tell me, please? Is there a Mr Rosenstein staying there?'

Tuppence shook her head. 'No. I'm afraid not. Perhaps he has been there and left. Will I ask for you?'

'No, no. I make mistake. Excuse, please.' Then she turned and walked quickly down the hill. Tuppence stood staring after her, feeling suspicious. But following the woman could make people think that Mrs Blenkensop was not who she appeared to be.

Inside, the house seemed very quiet and empty, which was usual early in the afternoon. Betty was having her sleep, the older residents were either resting or had gone out. Then a sound came to Tuppence's ears. The telephone at *Sans Souci* was in the hall. Tuppence heard the sound of someone lifting or replacing a <u>telephone extension</u>. There was only one extension – in Mrs Perenna's bedroom. Very carefully Tuppence lifted the telephone receiver in the hall and heard a man's voice.

'. . . everything going well. On the fourth, then, as arranged.'

'Yes, carry on,' a woman's voice replied.

There was a click as the telephone was replaced.

Tuppence stood, frowning. Was that Mrs Perenna's voice she had heard? It was difficult to say. There was movement behind her and Tuppence put down the receiver as Mrs Perenna spoke.

'It is such a pleasant afternoon. Are you going out, Mrs Blenkensop, or have you just come in?'

So it was not Mrs Perenna who had been in Mrs Perenna's room. Tuppence said something about having had a lovely walk and moved to the staircase.

Mrs Perenna moved along the hall after her. She seemed bigger than usual. Tuppence was conscious of her as a strong athletic woman.

She hurried up the stairs. As she turned the corner of the landing, she <u>collided</u> with Mrs O'Rourke, whose <u>vast</u> body blocked the top of the stairs.

'Dear, dear, Mrs Blenkensop, you seem to be in a great hurry.'

There was, as always, a frightening quality about Mrs O'Rourke's smile. And suddenly Tuppence felt afraid. The big smiling Irishwoman, with her deep voice, blocking her way, and below Mrs Perenna at the foot of the stairs.

And then suddenly the <u>tension</u> broke as a little figure ran along the top hall – little Betty Sprot shouting happily as she threw herself on Tuppence. The atmosphere had changed. Mrs O'Rourke, a big friendly figure, cried out, 'Ah, the darling!'

Below, Mrs Perenna had turned away to the door that led into the kitchen. And the atmosphere on the stairs, thought Tuppence, that tense moment, might have been just her own overactive nerves.

Chapter 5

Commander Haydock welcomed Tommy and Major Bletchley with enthusiasm and insisted on showing Mr Meadowes 'all over my little place'.

Smugglers' Rest had been two cottages standing on the cliff overlooking the sea. A London businessman had bought them and made them into one. There was a small cove below, but the path down to it was dangerous.

'Then, some years ago,' explained Haydock, '*Smugglers*' was sold to a man called Hahn. He was a German, and if you ask me, he was a spy. The Nazis are methodical. They were preparing even then for this war. Look at the situation of this place – it's perfect for sending signals out to sea. And there's a cove below where you could land a small boat without being seen. Oh yes, don't tell me that Hahn wasn't a German agent.

'He spent a lot of money on this place. He had a path made down to the beach – concrete steps – an expensive business. Then he had the whole of the house improved. And who did he get to do all this? Not a local man. No, it was a firm from London, or so they say – but a lot of the men who came down didn't speak a word of English. Don't you agree that that sounds extremely suspicious?'

'A little strange, certainly,' agreed Tommy.

'I was staying in the neighbourhood at the time and I used to watch the workmen. They didn't like it. Once or twice they were quite threatening. Why should they be if everything was okay? I went to the authorities. And what response did I get? "Another war with Germany was impossible," they insisted. There was peace in Europe – our relations with Germany were excellent. No one believed me when I said that the Germans were building the finest Air Force in Europe!'

Haydock's face was redder than usual with anger. 'They thought I was just trying to start another war. But finally I began to make an impression. We had a new Chief Constable down here – a retired soldier. And *he* listened to me. His men began to investigate and then Hahn left secretly one night. The police searched this place carefully. In a safe built into a wall in the dining-room, they found a wireless transmitter and big tanks under the garage for petrol. The end of the story was that I bought the place when it was put up for sale. Come and have a look round, Meadowes?'

'Thanks, I'd like to.'

Commander Haydock was as full of energy as a man half his age. He threw open the big safe in the dining room to show where the secret transmitter had been found. Tommy was taken out to the garage and was shown where the big petrol tanks had been hidden, and finally he was led down the steep path to the little cove and taken into the cave that had given the place its name because it was where the smugglers had hidden their goods.

More than ever now Tommy felt that when the dying Farquhar had mentioned *Sans Souci*, he had been on the right track. This part of the coast had been selected for enemy activity. His spirits rose. Although *Sans Souci* seemed an innocent place, behind the scenes things were going on.

★ ★ ★

Mrs Blenkensop was reading a letter on thin foreign paper stamped outside with the censor's mark. This was the direct result of her conversation with 'Mr Faraday'.

'Dear Raymond,' she said. 'I was so happy about him being out in Egypt, and now, it seems, there is a big change round.

All very secret, of course, and he can't say anything – just that there really is a marvellous plan and that I'm to be ready for some big surprise soon. I'm glad to know where he's being sent, but I . . .'

Bletchley frowned. 'Surely he's not allowed to tell you that?'

Tuppence looked round the breakfast table as she folded up her precious letter. 'Oh! We have our methods,' she said with a little laugh. 'Dear Raymond knows that if I know where he is, or where he's going, I don't worry quite so much. It's quite a simple code, too. Just a certain word, and after it the first letters of the next words spell out the place. I'm sure nobody would notice.'

Little murmurs arose round the table. The moment was well chosen; everybody was at the breakfast table together for once. Bletchley, his face red, said, 'Mrs Blenkensop, that's a very stupid thing to do. It's the movements of soldiers and airmen that are just what the Germans want to know.'

'Oh, but I never tell anyone!' cried Tuppence. 'And I'm very careful never to leave letters around. I always keep them locked up.'

Bletchley shook his head.

* * *

It was a grey morning with the wind blowing coldly from the sea. Tuppence was at the far end of the beach. As she reached the bottom of the cliff, her attention was caught by two figures standing talking a little way up. It was the same fair-haired woman she had seen the day before and Carl von Deinim. At that moment the young German turned his head and saw her. Immediately, the two figures parted. The woman came quickly down the hill and crossed the road.

Carl von Deinim waited until Tuppence came up to him. Then, politely, he wished her good morning.

Tuppence inquired immediately, 'Was that a friend you were talking to, Mr Deinim?'

'Not at all,' said Carl. 'She is Polish and asked me if I knew a Mrs Gottlieb she thinks lives near here. I do not, and she says she has, perhaps, got the name of the house wrong.'

'I see,' murmured Tuppence thoughtfully. Mr Rosenstein. Mrs Gottlieb. She felt a growing suspicion about the Polish woman.

That evening, before she went to bed, Tuppence pulled out the long drawer of her dressing table. At one side of it was a small box with a cheap lock. Tuppence put on gloves, unlocked the box, and opened it. A pile of letters lay inside. On the top was the one received that morning from 'Raymond'. Tuppence opened it again and frowned. She had placed an <u>eyelash</u> in the fold of the paper this morning. The eyelash was not there now.

Somebody was interested in the movements of the British armed forces.

★ ★ ★

Who had read her letters? Tuppence thought about it as she lay in bed the following morning. Her thoughts were interrupted by Betty Sprot who opened the door and ran in. Betty had taken a great liking to Tuppence. She climbed up on the bed and pushed a torn picture-book under Tuppence's nose, commanding her to 'read it'. Only she said 'wead' as she couldn't pronounce the letter 'r' yet. Tuppence read obediently.

'<u>Goosey goosey gander</u>, whither will you wander?
Upstairs, downstairs, in my lady's chamber.'

Betty rolled about with laughter – repeating in delight, 'Upstais – upstais – upstais . . .' and then 'Down . . .' and rolled off the bed with a <u>thump</u>.

This was repeated several times, then Betty <u>crawled</u> about the floor playing with Tuppence's shoes and talking busily to herself, 'Ag do – bah pit – soo – soodah – putch . . .' Then she looked up at Tuppence again and said, 'Ag boo bate? Ag boo bate?'

'Lovely, darling,' said Tuppence, not knowing what Betty was saying. 'Beautiful.'

Satisfied, Betty started talking to herself again and Tuppence lay planning what to do next – with Tommy's help. Suddenly Mrs Sprot came running in, looking for Betty.

'Oh, here she is! Oh, Betty, you <u>naughty</u> girl – Mrs Blenkensop, I am so sorry.'

Tuppence sat up in bed and looked at Betty who, with an innocent face, had removed the <u>laces</u> from Tuppence's shoes and put them in a glass of water. Tuppence laughed.

'How funny! Don't worry, Mrs Sprot, they'll be OK. It's my fault. I should have noticed what she was doing. She was rather quiet.'

'I know,' Mrs Sprot sighed. 'Whenever they're quiet, it's a bad sign.' Mrs Sprot carried Betty away and Tuppence got up to put her plan into action.

Chapter 6

That day Mrs Blenkensop received a letter from her son Douglas. Mrs Blenkensop was so excited that everybody at *Sans Souci* heard about it. The letter had not been censored at all, she explained, because one of Douglas's friends coming <u>on leave</u> had brought it, so Douglas had been able to write quite openly.

'And it just shows,' declared Mrs Blenkensop, 'how little we really know of what is going on.'

After breakfast she went upstairs to her room and put the letter away. Then she went downstairs again. She had already told everyone that she was going up to London for the day to see her lawyer and do a little shopping. And although she had no wish to do so, Mrs Blenkensop had said that she was going to London, and to London she must go.

★ ★ ★

It was not until the next day that Tuppence was able to have a meeting with Tommy. Mrs Blenkensop met Mr Meadowes as he was taking a walk on the beach.

'Well?' said Tuppence. 'Did you see anyone go into my room?'

Tommy nodded his head. 'The maids went in to clean the room, of course. And Mrs Perenna went in – but that was when the maids were there. And Betty ran in once and came out with a woollen dog.'

'Anyone else?'

'One person,' said Tommy slowly. 'Carl von Deinim. At lunchtime. He came out from the dining room early, came up to his room, then went across the passage and into yours. He was there about a quarter of an hour. That settles it, I think.'

Tuppence nodded. Yes, it was quite clear now. Carl von Deinim could have had no reason for going into Mrs Blenkensop's bedroom and remaining there for a quarter of an hour, except for one.

'I'm sorry,' she said slowly.

'So am I,' said Tommy. 'He's a nice boy.'

'Well, I think we can agree that Carl von Deinim is working with Sheila and her mother,' said Tuppence. 'Probably Mrs Perenna is in charge and that foreign woman who was talking to Carl yesterday must be involved somehow.'

'What do we do now?' Tommy asked.

'We must search Mrs Perenna's room. And we must follow her and see where she goes and who she meets. Tommy, let's get Albert down here.'

Many years ago Albert, who had worked in a hotel, had helped the young Beresfords. Afterwards he had gone to work for them as a general servant. Six years ago he had married and was now the proud owner of *The Duck and Dog*, a pub in South London.

Tuppence continued quickly, 'Albert will be really excited. He can stay at the pub near the station and he can follow the Perennas for us – or anyone else.'

'What about Mrs Albert?'

'She has gone to her mother's in Wales with the children because of possible air raids on London. It all fits in perfectly.'

'Yes, that's a good idea, Tuppence. Albert will be perfect. Now another thing – I think we ought to watch out for that so-called Polish woman who was talking to Carl. She probably comes here for orders, or to take messages. Next time we see her, one of us must follow her and find out more about her.'

* * *

Tommy continued his walk and entered the post office where he phoned Mr Grant. Then he wrote and sent a letter to Albert and bought himself a newspaper. He was walking back to *Sans Souci* when Commander Haydock, passing in his car, shouted, 'Hello, Meadowes, want a lift?'

Tommy got in gratefully.

'So you read that awful newspaper, do you?' demanded Haydock, looking at the red cover of the *Inside Weekly News*.

'It's terrible,' Tommy agreed. 'But sometimes they do seem to know what's going on behind the scenes.'

'The truth of it is,' said Commander Haydock, just missing a large van, 'when they're right, you remember it, and when they're wrong, you forget it. Do you feel like a game of golf tomorrow? I've got to go to a meeting about this Parashot business, getting together a group of local volunteers – good idea if you ask me. So, will we have a round of golf about six?'

'Thanks very much.'

'Good. Then that's agreed.' The Commander stopped abruptly at the gate of *Sans Souci*. 'How's the fair Sheila?' he asked.

'Quite well, I think. I haven't seen much of her.'

Haydock gave his loud laugh. 'Not as much as you'd like to, I bet! She's a good-looking girl but she sees too much of that German fellow. Unpatriotic, I call it.'

Mr Meadowes said, 'Be careful, he's just coming up the hill behind us.'

'I don't care if he does hear! Any *decent* German's fighting for his country – not running over here to avoid it!'

Chapter 7

On the following day Mrs Sprot went up to London. Various residents of *Sans Souci* had offered to look after Betty, and Tuppence had the morning turn.

'Play,' said Betty. 'Play hide seek.'

She was talking more easily every day and had <u>adopted</u> a most attractive habit of putting her head on one side with a lovely smile and murmuring 'Peese', which was her way of saying 'please'. Tuppence had intended to take her for a walk, but it was raining, so the two of them went into Mrs Sprot's bedroom. Betty led the way to the drawer of the bureau where her toys were kept.

'Shall we hide Bonzo?' asked Tuppence.

But Betty had changed her mind and demanded instead, 'Wead me story.'

Tuppence pulled out a book only to be interrupted by a cry from Betty.

'No, no. Bad . . .'

Tuppence stared at her in surprise and then down at the book, which was a coloured version of <u>Little Jack Horner</u>.

'Was Jack a bad boy?' she asked. 'Because he pulled out a <u>plum</u>?'

'B-a-ad!' Betty said, and then, with a huge effort, '<u>Nasty</u>!' She took the book from Tuppence and put it back, then took out an identical book from the other end of the shelf, saying with a huge smile, 'K-k-klean ni'tice Jackorner!'

Tuppence realised that any dirty, well-read books had been replaced by new and cleaner ones. Mrs Sprot was always terrified of <u>germs</u>. Tuppence had brought up her own two children in contact with a reasonable amount of dirt. However, she took the clean copy of *Jack Horner* and read it to the child, followed by another – *Goosey, Goosey, Gander.* Then Betty hid the books and Tuppence took an amazingly long time to find each of them, to Betty's great delight, and so the morning passed quickly.

After lunch Betty had her rest and it was then that Tuppence looked out into the garden and saw that the rain had stopped. At the bottom of the garden the bushes parted slightly. In the gap a face appeared. It was the Polish woman staring up at the windows of *Sans Souci.* The woman's face had no expression, and yet there was something frightening about it.

Turning abruptly from the window, Tuppence ran downstairs, out of the front door and down the path at the side of the house to where she had seen the woman. There was no one there now. Tuppence went through the bushes and out on to the road and looked up and down the hill. She could see no one. Troubled, she turned and went back into *Sans Souci.* Could she have imagined the whole thing? No, the woman had been there. She felt a strange sense that something bad was going to happen.

* * *

Now that the weather had improved, Miss Minton was taking Betty out for a walk. They were going down to the town to buy a toy duck to sail in Betty's bath. Betty was very excited and the two set off together, Betty saying happily, 'Byaduck. Byaduck. For Bettibarf. For Bettibarf.'

Two <u>matchsticks</u>, left crossed on the marble table in the hall, was the code that told Tuppence that Mr Meadowes was spending the afternoon following Mrs Perenna. Tuppence went to the lounge and sat with Mr and Mrs Cayley. Mr Cayley was unhappy. He had come to Leahampton, he explained, for rest and quiet, and what quiet could there be with a child in the house? All day long she was screaming and running about, jumping up and down.

His wife murmured that Betty was really 'a dear little girl', but the comment only annoyed him more.

'No doubt, no doubt,' said Mr Cayley. 'But her mother should keep her quiet. There are other people to consider. Invalids, people who need to rest.'

Quickly, Tuppence changed the subject. 'I wish you would tell me your views on life in Germany. You've travelled there several times and it would be interesting to have your point of view . . .'

Mr Cayley smiled. 'Dear lady, in my opinion . . .'

Tuppence, murmuring an occasional 'Now that's very interesting,' listened with close attention. She was quickly convinced that Mr Cayley was an admirer of the Nazi system. He clearly thought, though he did not say it openly, how much better it would have been if England and Germany had taken sides against the rest of Europe.

Nearly two hours later they were interrupted by the return of Miss Minton, Betty, and the duck. Looking up, Tuppence caught a strange expression on Mrs Cayley's face. It might have been simply a wife's jealousy at her husband paying so much attention to another woman. It might have been concern that Mr Cayley was speaking too clearly about his political views. It certainly expressed dissatisfaction.

Tea came next and soon after that came the return of Mrs Sprot from London exclaiming, 'I do hope Betty's been good?'

Mrs Sprot then sat down, drank several cups of tea, and spoke excitedly about what she had bought in London, the crowd on the train, what a soldier recently returned from France had told the people in her train carriage, and what a girl in a shop had told her of <u>shortages</u> to come.

The conversation was, in fact, completely normal. It went on afterwards on the terrace outside, for the sun was now shining.

Betty rushed happily about, going into the bushes and returning with a leaf, or little stones which she placed in the lap of one of the grown-ups. She would give an explanation in her own little language, which no one could understand, of what they represented. Fortunately she required little response in her game, being satisfied with an occasional, 'How nice, darling. Is it really?'

There had never been an evening more typical of *Sans Souci*. There was talk about the war – Can France fight back? What is Russia likely to do? Could Hitler invade England if he tried? Will Paris fall to the Germans?

Suddenly, Mrs Sprot glanced at her watch. 'Goodness, it's nearly seven. I ought to have put that child to bed ages ago. Betty, Betty!'

It was some time since Betty had returned to the terrace, though no one had really noticed. Mrs Sprot called her with growing impatience.

'Bett-eeee! Where can the child be?'

Mrs O'Rourke said with her deep laugh, 'Doing something naughty, I've no doubt about it. It's always the way when there's quiet.'

'Betty! I want you.' There was no answer and Mrs Sprot rose impatiently. 'I suppose I must go and look for her. I wonder where she can be?'

Miss Minton suggested that she was hiding somewhere, but Betty could not be found, either inside or outside the house. They went round the garden calling and they looked in all the bedrooms. There was no Betty anywhere.

Mrs Sprot began to get annoyed. 'It's very naughty of her – very naughty indeed! Do you think she can have gone out on the road?'

Together she and Tuppence went out to the gate and looked up and down the hill. There was no one in sight except a delivery boy with a bicycle standing talking to a maid at the door of the house across the road. Tuppence and Mrs Sprot crossed the road and Mrs Sprot asked if either of them had seen a little girl. The maid asked, 'A little girl in a green dress?'

Mrs Sprot replied eagerly, 'That's right.'

'I saw her about half an hour ago – going down the road with a woman.'

Mrs Sprot said with amazement, 'With a woman? What sort of a woman?'

The girl seemed slightly embarrassed. 'Well, what I'd call a strange-looking woman. I'm sure she was foreign. She was wearing strange clothes, like a kind of <u>shawl</u>, and no hat. Her face was strange too. I've seen her about once or twice lately, and to tell the truth I thought she was a bit mad.'

Mrs Sprot almost <u>collapsed</u> against Tuppence. 'Oh Betty, my little girl. She's been stolen. She – what did the woman look like – was she dark?'

Tuppence shook her head energetically. 'No, she was fair, very fair, with a wide face and blue eyes set very far apart.' She saw Mrs Sprot staring at her and hurried to explain, 'I've noticed her around here. Carl von Deinim was speaking to her one day. It must be the same woman.'

The servant girl agreed. 'That's right. Fair-haired she was.'

'Oh,' cried Mrs Sprot. 'What shall I do?'

Tuppence put an arm round her. 'Come back to the house, have a little brandy and then we'll ring up the police. It's all right. We'll get her back.'

Mrs Sprot cried out weakly, 'She's some dreadful German woman, I expect. She'll kill my Betty.'

'Nonsense,' said Tuppence. 'It will be all right. I expect she's just some woman who's not quite right in her head.' But she did not believe her own words – she did not believe for one moment that the calm blonde woman was mad.

'Carl!' thought Tuppence, 'Would Carl know? Had he had anything to do with this?' However, a few minutes later she started to doubt this <u>assumption</u>. Carl von Deinim, like the rest, seemed completely surprised. As soon as the facts were told, Major Bletchley took control.

'Now then, dear lady,' he said to Mrs Sprot. 'Sit down here and just drink a little of this brandy. I'll contact the police station immediately.'

Mrs Sprot murmured, 'Wait a minute – there might be something . . .' She hurried up the stairs and along the passage to her room. A minute or two later they heard her footsteps running along the upstairs hall. She rushed down the stairs and took Major Bletchley's hand from the telephone receiver, which he was just about to lift.

'No, no, you mustn't – you mustn't . . .' And crying wildly, she collapsed into a chair.

They crowded round her. In a minute or two, she recovered herself. Sitting up, with Mrs Cayley's arm round her, she held something out for them to see. 'I found this on the floor of my room. It had been wrapped round a stone and thrown through the window. Look – look what it says.'

Tommy took it from her and unfolded it. It was a note, written in big, bold letters.

> WE HAVE GOT YOUR CHILD. SHE IS SAFE. YOU WILL BE TOLD WHAT TO DO SOON. IF YOU GO TO THE POLICE, YOUR CHILD WILL BE KILLED. SAY NOTHING.

Mrs Sprot was repeating faintly, 'Betty – Betty.'

Everyone was talking at once.

'The dirty murdering criminals,' exclaimed Mrs O'Rourke.

'<u>Brutes</u>!' shouted Sheila Perenna.

'I don't believe a word of it. It's a silly practical joke,' declared Mr Cayley.

'Oh, the dear little girl!' murmured Miss Minton.

'I do not understand. It is shocking,' added Carl von Deinim.

And above everyone else the loud voice of Major Bletchley. 'We *must* inform the police at once. They'll soon find out what's going on.'

Once more he moved towards the telephone. This time a scream from Mrs Sprot stopped him.

He shouted, 'But my dear Madam, we must. This note is only to stop you doing anything so that they can get away.'

'They'll kill her.'

'Nonsense! They wouldn't dare.'

'I won't allow it, I tell you. I'm her mother. It's for me to say.'

'I know. I know. That's what they're counting on – your feeling like that. It's very natural. But you must believe me, I'm a soldier and an experienced man of the world. The police are what we need.'

'No!'

Bletchley's eyes went round, searching for agreement.

'Meadowes, you agree with me?' Slowly Tommy nodded.

'Cayley?' Mr Cayley nodded too.

'Look, Mrs Sprot, both Meadowes and Cayley agree.'

Mrs Sprot said with sudden energy, 'Men! All of you! Ask the women!'

Tommy looked at Tuppence who said, her voice low and shaken, 'I – I agree with Mrs Sprot.'

She was thinking of her own children. 'Deborah! Derek! If it were them, I'd feel like her. Tommy and the others are right, I've no doubt, but I couldn't do it. I couldn't risk it,' she said to herself.

Mrs O'Rourke was declaring, 'No mother alive could risk it and that's a fact.'

Miss Minton said weakly, 'Such awful things happen. We'd never forgive ourselves if anything happened to dear little Betty.'

'You haven't said anything, Mr von Deinim?' noted Tuppence sharply.

Carl's blue eyes were very bright. His face had no expression. He said slowly, 'I am a foreigner. I do not know your English police. How good they are – how quick.'

Someone had come into the hall. It was Mrs Perenna, her cheeks were red. Evidently she had been hurrying up the hill. 'What's all this?' she asked. Her voice was commanding, not the pleasant guesthouse owner, but a woman of force.

They told her – a confused story told by too many people, but she understood it quickly. She held the note for a minute, then she handed it back. Her words were sharp and <u>authoritative</u>.

'The police? They'll be no good. You can't risk their making mistakes. Go after the child yourselves.'

Bletchley said, 'Very well.'

Tommy added, 'They can't be far away. When did it happen?'

'Half an hour, the maid said,' Tuppence answered.

'Haydock,' said Bletchley. 'Haydock's the man to help us. He's got a car. The woman's unusual looking, you say? And a foreigner? She ought to leave a <u>trail</u> that we can follow. Come on, there's no time to lose. You'll come along, Meadowes?'

Mrs Sprot got up. 'I'm coming, too.'

'Now, my dear lady, leave it to us . . .'
'I'm coming, too.'
'Oh, well.' He gave in.

★ ★ ★

Commander Haydock, who understood the situation immediately, drove the car. Tommy sat beside him, and behind were Bletchley, Mrs Sprot and Tuppence. Not only did Mrs Sprot cling to her, but Tuppence was the only one (with the exception of Carl von Deinim) who knew the mysterious <u>kidnapper</u> by sight.

The Commander was a good organizer and a quick worker. In minutes he had filled up the car with petrol, handed Bletchley a map of the district and a larger map of Leahampton itself and was ready to start off.

Mrs Sprot had run upstairs again before they left, presumably to get a coat. But when she got into the car and they had started down the hill, she showed Tuppence something in her handbag. It was a small <u>pistol</u>.

She explained quietly, 'I got it from Major Bletchley's room. I remember he said he had one.'

Tuppence looked a little uncertain. 'You don't think that . . .?'

Mrs Sprot said, her mouth a thin line, 'It may be useful.'

Tuppence sat wondering about the strength of a mother's love for a child, even in an ordinary young woman. She could see Mrs Sprot, the type of woman who would normally be frightened to death of guns, calmly shooting any person who had harmed her child.

They drove first, on the Commander's suggestion, to the railway station. A train had left Leahampton about twenty minutes earlier and it was possible that the woman and Betty and whoever else was involved had travelled on it. At the station they separated, the Commander questioned the ticket collector, Tommy asked the ticket office staff, and Bletchley checked with the porters outside. Tuppence and Mrs Sprot went into the ladies' bathroom just in case the woman had gone in there to change her appearance before taking the train.

None of them discovered anything.

'The kidnappers probably had a car waiting,' Haydock suggested, 'and they made their escape in that.'

Tuppence remarked, 'We must put ourselves in their places. Where would they have waited in the car? Somewhere as near as *Sans Souci* as possible, but where a car wouldn't be noticed. Now let's think . . . The woman and Betty walk down the hill together. At the bottom is the esplanade. The car might have been waiting there.'

It was at that moment that a small man stepped up to them and said, 'Excuse me, I couldn't help overhearing what you were asking the porter just now.'

He directed his remarks to Major Bletchley. 'I was not listening, of course, just came down to see about a parcel and so, you see, I happened to overhear – and really it did seem the most wonderful coincidence . . .'

Mrs Sprot sprang forward. She took him by the arm. 'You've seen her? You've seen my little girl?'

'Oh really, *your* little girl, you say? Now . . .'

Mrs Sprot cried, 'Tell me!'

Tuppence interrupted calmly, 'Please tell us anything you have seen as quickly as you can. We will be most grateful if you would.'

'Oh, well, really, of course, it may be nothing at all. But the description fitted so well . . .'

Tuppence felt the woman beside her trembling, but she herself tried to stay calm. She knew the type of man with whom they were dealing — not capable of giving a direct answer, especially if hurried. 'Please tell us,' she repeated.

Tuppence frowned at Major Bletchley, who was about to start shouting at him, and asked, 'And you saw the little girl we are looking for?'

'Yes, I really think it must be. A little girl with a foreign-looking woman, you said? It was really the woman I noticed. Because, of course, we are all on the lookout nowadays for Fifth Columnists, aren't we? So, as I say, I noticed this woman. A nurse, I thought, or a maid, and this woman was most unusual looking and walking up the road to the hills beside the sea. She was with a little girl — and the little girl seemed tired and it was half-past seven, and well, most children go to bed then. I looked at the woman very closely and she hurried up the road, pulling the child after her. Finally she picked her up and went on up the path out on to the cliff, which I thought strange. There are no houses there at all — nothing — not until you get to Whitehaven — about five miles away.'

Commander Haydock was back in the car and had started the engine. The others jumped in.

Tuppence called out, 'Thank you,' and they drove off, leaving him staring after them with his mouth open.

They drove quickly through the town, avoiding accidents more by good luck than by skill. The road ended on bare hillside where there was only a footpath.

'Better get out and walk here,' said Bletchley.

Haydock suggested, 'Why don't we take the car up? The ground's firm enough.'

Mrs Sprot cried, 'Oh yes, please, please. We must be quick.'

The car <u>bounced</u> about as it went across the rough ground but they arrived without any problem on the top of the hill. Here the view was clear.

'No sign of them as far as I can see,' observed Haydock.

He was standing up, looking through some <u>binoculars</u> that he had brought with him. Suddenly he focused on two small moving figures.

'Got 'em!'

He fell back into the driver's seat again and now the chase was a short one. Bounced up in the air, thrown from side to side as the car drove over the uneven ground, the occupants of the car quickly got closer to those two small figures. They could see them clearly now – a woman holding a child by the hand – still nearer, yes, a child in a green dress. Betty.

Suddenly the woman turned and saw the car advancing towards her. With a cry she picked up the child in her arms and began running towards the edge of the cliff.

The car could not follow; the ground was now too uneven and blocked with big stones. It stopped and Mrs Sprot was out first running towards them. The others followed her. When they were within twenty <u>yards</u> of her, the kidnapper turned. She was standing at the very edge of the cliff and with a cry, she held the child closer to herself.

Haydock exclaimed, 'No! She's going to throw the kid over the cliff . . .'

The woman's face was filled with hate. She spoke, a long angry sentence that none of them understood. And still she held the child and looked from time to time at the sea below. It seemed clear that she was threatening to throw the child over the cliff. All of them stood there, confused and terrified, unable to move for fear of causing a catastrophe.

Haydock's hand was in his pocket. He pulled out a pistol and shouted, 'Put that child down – or I fire.'

The foreign woman laughed.

Haydock whispered, 'I can't shoot. I might hit the child.'

Tommy cried, 'The woman's crazy. She'll jump over the edge with the child in another moment.'

Haydock said again, helplessly, 'It's too dangerous to shoot...'

But at that moment a shot rang out. The woman fell back, the child still in her arms. The men ran forward, Mrs Sprot stood still, the smoking pistol in her hands, her eyes wide open. She took a few steps forward. Tommy was kneeling by the bodies. He turned them over gently. The woman was dead – shot through the head. Unhurt, little Betty Sprot stood up and ran towards her mother who was standing completely still.

Then, at last, Mrs Sprot moved. She threw away the pistol and fell to her knees, holding the child to her. 'She's safe – she's safe – oh, Betty – Betty.' And then, in a low whisper she added, 'Did I – did I – kill her?'

Tuppence said firmly, 'Don't think about it. Think about Betty. Just think about Betty.'

Mrs Sprot held the child close against her, crying uncontrollably. Tuppence went forward to join the men.

Haydock said, 'I couldn't have managed a shot like that! I don't believe the woman has ever used a pistol before – it must have been pure <u>instinct</u>. A miracle, that's what it is.'

Tuppence murmured, 'It was a near thing!' And she looked down at the sea far below and <u>shivered</u>.

Chapter 8

The police identified the dead woman as Vanda Polonska, a Polish refugee, and the inquest on her death opened with the formal identification of the body by a Mrs Calfont, who worked with refugees. Polonska, she said, had come to England with a cousin and his wife who were her only relatives. She had experienced great horror in Poland and her family, including several children, had all been killed. Polonska talked to herself constantly, and did not seem normal.

The coroner asked why the woman's relatives were not present, and at this point an Inspector Brassey said that the couple had been arrested for a crime at a Naval dockyard. The whole family was considered suspicious. They had had a large sum of money in their possession, which they could not explain, but there was no evidence against Polonska – except that her opinions were believed to have been anti-British. It was possible that she had been an enemy agent. The verdict was that Vanda Polonska had been killed by Mrs Sprot but that Betty's mother should not be blamed.

★ ★ ★

The following day Mrs Blenkensop and Mr Meadowes met.

'Goodbye Vanda Polonska,' said Tommy sadly.

Tuppence nodded. 'Yes, and nothing to tell us who she was working for and no clues about where the money came from that she and her cousins had.'

'Do you think Carl von Deinim and Vanda Polonska were working together?' asked Tommy.

'Yes,' said Tuppence.

'Then Carl von Deinim must have arranged the kidnapping – but why kidnap Betty? The Sprots have no money – so it wasn't for <u>ransom</u>, and neither of them are employed by government.'

'I know, Tommy. It just doesn't make any sense at all. But I've a feeling that Mrs Sprot could find the reason if only she'd think about it. There must be some piece of information that she discovered without knowing what it was.'

'"Say nothing. Wait for instructions",' Tommy quoted from the note found on Mrs Sprot's bedroom floor. 'That *means* something.'

'The only thing I can think of is that Mrs Sprot, or her husband, has been given something to keep by someone else. And they were given it simply because they are such ordinary people that no one would ever suspect they had it – whatever "it" may be.'

'Have you asked Mrs Sprot to think about why Betty was taken?'

'Yes, but all she cares about is having Betty back – that, and having <u>hysterics</u> because she shot someone.'

'Funny creatures, women,' commented Tommy. 'I wouldn't have risked firing when she did.'

'She wouldn't have either if she'd known more about it. It was her complete <u>ignorance</u> of the difficulty of the shot that made her do it. But you know, the first time I saw Vanda Polonska, her face seemed vaguely familiar. I wish I could remember who she reminded me of.'

* * *

At *Sans Souci*, Tuppence went straight upstairs to her room where a tall figure turned away from the window.

'Sheila?' said Tuppence.

The girl's face was completely white. 'They've arrested Carl! What shall I do?'

'Oh, my dear.'

'They've taken him away. I'll never see him again. What shall I do? What shall I do?' And falling on her knees, she started to cry.

Tuppence stroked Sheila's dark head. 'Perhaps they are only going to intern him.'

'That's not what they said. They're searching his room now.'

Tuppence said slowly, 'Well, if they find nothing . . .'

'*What* might they find?'

'I don't know. I thought perhaps you might have an idea?'

'Me?'

Her amazement was real. Any suspicions Tuppence had had that Sheila Perenna was involved in spying, died. She continued, 'If he is innocent . . .'

'What does it matter?' Sheila interrupted her. 'The police will make up a false case against him and say he was working for the Germans.'

Tuppence said sharply, 'My dear child, that isn't true.'

'The English police will do anything. My mother says so. They'll take him away and lock him up, and one morning they'll stand him against a wall and shoot him!'

★ ★ ★

The fisherman on the end of the pier said to Mr Meadowes, 'There's no doubt whatever, I'm afraid.' Mr Grant said. 'Among his papers was a list of people where he worked who should be approached, as possible Fascist sympathisers. There was also a very clever idea to mix chemicals into fertilisers, which would have destroyed food crops. He also had a supply of invisible ink.

I've only seen the method once before, and then it was buttons which had been soaked in the stuff. When the fellow wanted to use it, he soaked a button in water. Carl von Deinim's invisible ink wasn't in his buttons, it was in his shoelaces.'

As soon as Tommy reported this conversation to Tuppence, she cried, 'Tommy, that explains it!'

'What?'

'Betty! Don't you remember what I told you she did in my room, taking out my shoelaces and soaking them in water? She must have seen Carl do it! He couldn't risk her talking about it, and so he arranged with that woman for her to be kidnapped. Isn't it nice when things begin to make sense? Now we can move forward.'

'We need to.'

Tuppence nodded. The news from France was very bad indeed. The British Expeditionary Force was being pushed back by the Germans and now the talk of an invasion of Britain had a frightening reality.

Tommy said, 'I think that Carl von Deinim was only a link in the chain, not N or M who are probably the most important German agents in England. So is Mrs Perenna M? And do you really think her daughter isn't involved in this, Tuppence?'

'I'm quite sure of it.'

'First, the man she loves is proved to be a spy – and if her mother is also one, she's not going to have much left, is she? And supposing we're wrong – that M or N is someone else? I've got some other ideas, you know.'

'Which are?'

'I think I'll keep them to myself for a bit. We'll see which of us is right.'

'Well, I think we've got to find out where Mrs Perenna goes, who she meets – everything. You'd better tell our old friend Albert to follow her this afternoon. He'll be glad to have something to do at last!'

'You can do that. I'm busy.'

'Why, what are you doing?'

Tommy said, 'I'm playing golf.'

Chapter 9

'It seems quite like old times, doesn't it, Madam?' said Albert. He smiled happily.

Tuppence asked about his wife.

'Oh, she's all right – just doesn't like being away from London and me, she says.'

'I'm not sure we should involve you in this adventure, Albert,' worried Tuppence.

'Nonsense, Madam. I tried to join the Army but they said, "Wait for people your age to be called up." And me, perfectly fit and only too eager to get at those Germans! Fifth Column, that's what we're up against, so the newspapers say – and I'm ready to assist you and Captain Beresford in any way you need me to.'

'Good. Now I'll tell you what we want you to do . . .'

* * *

After their game of golf, Tommy went to have supper with Commander Haydock at *Smugglers' Rest*. A tall, middle-aged manservant served them with the skill of a restaurant waiter. When the man had left the room, Tommy complimented the Commander on him.

'Yes, I was lucky to get Appledore.'

'How *did* you get him?'

'He answered an advertisement. He had excellent references, was far better than any of the others who applied for the job and asked for very low wages. So of course I hired him immediately.'

Tommy laughed, 'The war has certainly robbed us of much of our good restaurant service. Most good waiters were foreigners. It doesn't seem to come naturally to Englishmen.'

'Acting like a servant doesn't come easily to the English bulldog,' said the Commander, and went on to say that there would be a successful German invasion in the near future.

'There's no organization here, no proper co-ordination . . .'

Appledore brought whisky while the Commander was talking.

'. . . and there are spies everywhere. It was the same in the last war – foreign hairdressers, waiters . . .'

Tommy thought, 'Waiters? Appledore speaks perfect English, but many Germans do.'

'All these forms to fill in, with idiotic questions . . .' continued the Commander.

Tommy spoke on an impulse – the words fitted perfectly with what the Commander was just saying. 'I know, such as "What is your name?" Answer N or M.'

There was a crash as Appledore dropped a glass. Tommy's hand was soaked in whisky. The man stammered, 'S – Sorry, sir.'

Haydock was very angry and shouted at Appledore, 'You clumsy fool! What do you think you're doing?' Haydock continued for some minutes with more angry words. Tommy was embarrassed for Appledore, but suddenly the Commander's anger passed.

'Come along and wash that whisky off, Meadowes.'

Tommy was soon in the luxurious bathroom. He washed his hands, then turned from the washbasin to dry them. He didn't notice that a bar of soap had dropped on to the floor. His foot stepped on it and a moment later he skidded across the floor, arms outstretched. One hand came up against the right-hand tap of the bath, the other pushed heavily against the side of a small bathroom cabinet and his foot hit the end panel of the bath. Immediately the bath slid out from the wall and Tommy found himself looking into a cupboard that contained a wireless transmitter.

The Commander appeared in the doorway. And several things fell into place in Tommy's brain. Had he been blind? That cheerful red face was a mask. It was really the face of an arrogant Prussian officer. He remembered from long ago seeing a Prussian <u>bully</u> shouting at a soldier just as Commander Haydock had shouted at Appledore.

And it all fitted in. The enemy agent Hahn had been sent first in order to prepare *Smugglers' Rest*. He then drew attention to himself, allowing Commander Haydock to unmask him. How natural that Haydock should buy the place and then tell the story to everyone he met! And so N, securely settled in his place with his secret transmitter and his helpers at *Sans Souci*, was ready to carry out Germany's plan.

Tommy knew that he was in deadly danger unless he could act the part of the stupid Englishman well enough. He turned to Haydock with a laugh. '<u>By Jove</u>, was this another of Hahn's little <u>gadgets</u>? You didn't show me this the other day.'

Haydock stood as though made of stone for a minute, then he relaxed. 'Damned funny, Meadowes. You went skating over the floor like a ballet dancer!'

With an arm round Tommy's shoulders, Haydock took him into the sitting room. Half an hour later Mr Meadowes stood up.

'I really must be going now – it's getting quite late . . .'

Still talking, Mr Meadowes walked towards the door. He was in the hall . . . he opened the front door . . . They were going to let him get away with it! The two men stood talking, arranging another golf match for Saturday.

Tommy thought angrily, 'There'll be no next Saturday for you, Haydock – or whatever your real name is!'

Voices came from the road. Two men returning from a walk, men Tommy and the Commander knew who played at the golf club. Tommy called to them. They stopped for a few words with Haydock, then Tommy walked off with them.

He had managed to escape! It was so lucky that these men had come along. Tommy said goodbye to them at the gate of *Sans Souci* and walked up the drive whistling softly. He had just turned the dark corner by some large bushes when something heavy came down on his head and he fell into blackness . . .

★ ★ ★

At breakfast the next morning, Tuppence was aware of a tension in the atmosphere before Mrs Perenna left the room.

Major Bletchley gave a deep laugh. 'Mrs Perenna is in a very bad mood,' he remarked. 'Meadowes has been out all night. Hasn't come home yet.'

'What?' exclaimed Tuppence.

'Oh dear,' said Miss Minton, her face reddening.

Mrs Cayley looked shocked. Mrs O'Rourke merely grinned.

'Ah, well, boys will be boys.'

Tuppence tried to reassure herself. She and Tommy had agreed that neither should be worried if the other was absent for no apparent reason. She was sure that he would communicate with her, or just arrive, very soon.

In the evening, Mrs Perenna reluctantly agreed to ring up the police. A sergeant arrived and certain facts were noted. Mr Meadowes had left Commander Haydock's house at half-past ten. From there he had walked with Mr Walters and Dr Curtis to the gate of *Sans Souci*. From that moment, Mr Meadowes had disappeared.

Tuppence knew that Mrs Perenna had, according to Mrs Sprot, been out last night, and she believed her to be the most likely suspect in Tommy's disappearance. But Sheila and Major Bletchley had been at the cinema, though separately, and the way that he had insisted on describing the whole film might suggest to a suspicious mind that he was establishing an <u>alibi</u>. And Mr Cayley had gone for a walk round the garden and had been out for some time. It was very unlike him to risk being out in the cool night air . . . so, was he really as ill as he claimed?

★ ★ ★

Many miles away, at a secret Intelligence location, Tuppence Beresford's daughter was sitting at her desk frowning.

'What's the matter, Deborah? You're looking worried.'

Deborah Beresford looked up at Tony Marsdon. He was one of the most brilliant beginners in the coding department.

'It's my mother. I'm a bit worried about her. She was annoyed because nobody seemed to want her in this war. So she went down to Cornwall to stay with an aunt. But I told Charles, my boyfriend, who was going down to see his parents who live in Cornwall, to go and visit her. And he did. And she wasn't there.'

'Wasn't there?'

'No. And she hadn't been there! Not at all!'

'Where's – I mean – your father?'

'Oh, he's in Scotland somewhere.'

'Maybe your mother's gone to join him.'

'She can't. He's in one of those secret areas where wives can't go.'

'Oh – er – well, I suppose she's just gone away somewhere.'

'But why? It's so strange. She's been sending me letters – talking about her aunt and her garden and everything.'

'I know, I know,' said Tony hastily. 'Of course, she'd want you to think – I mean – nowadays – well, people do go away now and again if you know what I mean . . .'

'No! If you think Mother's just gone away with someone, you're wrong. Mother and Father are <u>devoted</u> to each other – really devoted. But the odd thing is that the other day someone said they'd seen Mother in Leahampton. I said it couldn't be her because she was in Cornwall, but now I wonder.'

'Leahampton?'

'Yes. It's the last place Mother would go to. There's nothing to do there and only old colonels and unmarried ladies live there.'

'Doesn't sound a likely place,' said Tony. He lit a cigarette and asked casually, 'What did your mother do in the last war?'

'She was a nurse.'

'I thought perhaps she'd been like you – in British Intelligence.'

'Oh, Mother would never have been able to do this sort of work although she and Father did get involved in searching for secret papers and spies at one point. Of course, they exaggerate it and make it all sound as though it had been very important.'

On the following day Deborah returned to her rooms and was puzzled by something unfamiliar in the appearance of her bedroom. It took her a few minutes to discover what it was. Then she rang the bell and asked her landlady what had happened to the big photograph that stood on the chest of drawers.

Mrs Rowley said she hadn't touched it. Maybe it had been Gladys, the maid.

But Gladys also denied having removed it. A man who'd come about the gas had been in Deborah's room she said. But Deborah refused to believe that an employee of the Gas Company would have stolen the photograph. It was more likely, in Deborah's opinion, that Gladys had accidentally broken the photograph frame and had hidden it in the rubbish bin.

Deborah didn't worry about it. She'd get her mother to send her another photo of herself.

Chapter 10

It was Tuppence's turn to talk to the fisherman on the end of the pier. She had hoped that Mr Grant might have had some comfort for her. But no news of any kind had come from Tommy.

Trying her best to make her voice assured and business-like, Tuppence said, 'I continue, of course.'

'Of course. There will be time for tears after the battle. We're in the middle of the battle now. And time is short. One piece of information you brought us has been proved correct. You overheard a reference to the 'fourth' when you listened to that telephone conversation in the hall at *Sans Souci*. The fourth referred to is the fourth of next month. It's the date fixed for the big attack on this country.'

'You're sure?'

'Yes, the fourth is The Day.'

'But if you know that –'

'We know The Day. We know, or think we know, where. We're as ready as we can be. But it's the Fifth Column *here* we want to know about. A dozen men in high places, in command of troops in vital areas, can issue conflicting orders and throw the country into a state of confusion. This is necessary for the German plan to succeed. We've got to have inside information in time.

'We have received information that Mrs Perenna is a member of the IRA with anti-British sympathies. But we can't get proof. So keep going, Mrs Beresford. Go on, and do your best.'

'The fourth,' said Tuppence. 'That's barely a week ahead!'

'It's a week exactly.'

She frowned and began planning a new form of attack.

★ ★ ★

'You see, Albert, it's a possibility,' Tuppence said a few hours later.

'I see what you mean, Madam, of course. But I don't like the idea very much, I must say.'

'I think it might work.'

'Yes, Madam, but it's exposing yourself to attack – that's what I don't like – and I'm sure Mr Beresford wouldn't like it either.'

'Albert, we've done what we could, staying hidden. It seems to me that now the only chance is to come out into the open.'

'How were you thinking of managing it, Madam?'

Tuppence said, 'I thought I might lose a letter I'd written – make a lot of <u>fuss</u> about it, seem very upset. Then it would be found in the hall and Beatrice would probably put it on the table. Then the right person would take a look at it.'

'What would be in the letter?'

'Oh, that I'd been successful in discovering the identity of the person in question and that I was to make a full report personally tomorrow. Then, you see, Albert, N or M would have to come out in the open and try to kill me.'

'Yes, and maybe they'd manage it, too.'

'Not if I was <u>on my guard</u>. They'd have, I think, to trick me into going to some <u>isolated</u> place. That's where your part would come in – because they don't know about you.'

★ ★ ★

Tuppence was just leaving the local library when she was startled by a voice calling, 'Mrs Beresford!'

She turned to see a tall dark young man with a slightly embarrassed smile.

'Do you remember me?' he asked. 'I came to the flat with Deborah one day.'

Deborah's friends! There were so many of them, and all looked very alike to Tuppence! It was annoying to have been recognised by one of Deborah's young men just now.

'I'm Anthony Marsdon,' explained the young man.

Tuppence murmured, 'Oh, of course,' and shook hands.

Tony Marsdon went on, 'I'm very glad to have found you, Mrs Beresford. You see, I'm working at the same job as Deborah, and something very <u>awkward</u> has happened.'

'Yes?' said Tuppence. 'What is it?'

'Well, you see, Deborah's found out that you're not down in Cornwall as she thought, and that makes it a bit awkward, doesn't it, for you?'

'Oh, no,' said Tuppence concerned. 'How did she find out?'

Tony Marsdon explained. He went on, 'Deborah, of course, has no idea of what you're really doing and it's important that she shouldn't know. My job, you see, is the same as yours. I'm supposed to be a beginner in the coding department. In fact, my instructions are to express views that are mildly Fascist – admiration of the German system, suggestions that an <u>alliance</u> with Hitler wouldn't be a bad thing – just to see what response I get. There's a good deal of dangerous talk like that going on, you see, and we want to find out who's behind it.'

'Dangerous talk everywhere,' thought Tuppence.

'But as soon as Deb told me about you,' continued the young man, 'I thought I'd better come straight down and warn you so that you can make up a story she'll believe. You see, I happen to know what you are doing and that it's of vital importance. It would be fatal if any <u>hint</u> of who you are was discovered. I thought perhaps you could pretend you'd joined Captain Beresford in Scotland or wherever he is. You might say to Deborah that you'd been allowed to work with him there.'

'I might do that, certainly,' said Tuppence thoughtfully.

Tony Marsdon said <u>anxiously</u>, 'You don't think I'm <u>interfering</u>?'

'No, no, I'm very grateful to you.'

'I'm – well – you see – I'm rather fond of Deborah,' admitted Tony.

Tuppence smiled at him. After a moment or two she said slowly, 'My husband isn't in Scotland.'

'Isn't he?'

'No, he's down here with me. At least he was! Now – he's disappeared.'

'Oh, that's bad – or isn't it? Has he discovered something?'

Tuppence nodded. 'I think so. That's why I don't think that his disappearance is really a bad sign. I think, sooner or later, he'll communicate with me – in his own way.' She smiled a little.

Tony said, with some embarrassment, 'Of course, you know how all of this works, I expect. But you ought to be careful.'

Tuppence nodded. 'I know what you mean. Beautiful heroines in books are always easily tricked. But Tommy and I have our methods. We've got a saying,' she smiled. 'Penny plain and <u>tuppence</u> coloured.'

'What?' The young man stared at her as though she had gone mad.

'I ought to explain that my family nickname is "Tuppence" – I won't go into why! So when Tommy and I want the other to know a letter is definitely from one of us, we use at least part of that old phrase, sometimes spelling "plain" as Playne. Originally you know, it referred to the <u>cardboard</u> scenes made for toy theatres which were very popular with families who put on the plays at home. You could buy plain scenes for a penny, but coloured ones cost tuppence.'

'Oh, I see.' The young man grinned. 'Very clever!'

'I hope so.'

'Can I help in any way?'

'Yes,' said Tuppence thoughtfully. 'I think perhaps you can.'

Chapter 11

After long hours of <u>unconsciousness</u>, Tommy woke up with an aching head. Slowly he became aware of other things – of cold, stiff arms and legs, of hunger, of not being able to move his lips. And that his head was resting on solid stone. Yes, he was lying on hard stones, and he was in pain, unable to move, extremely hungry, cold and uncomfortable. Surely, although Mrs Perenna's beds had never been soft, this could not be . . . Then he remembered. Of course – Haydock! The transmitter! The German waiter! Turning in at the gates of *Sans Souci* . . . Someone had struck him down. So Haydock hadn't been quite such a fool! Either he'd followed him or maybe Appledore had.

His eyes, accustomed to the darkness, could just see a small rectangle of pale light. A tiny window, slightly open. It was cold and the air smelt damp. He was, he thought, lying in a <u>cellar</u>. His hands and feet were tied and there was a <u>gag</u> in his mouth secured by a <u>bandage</u>.

'I'm really in trouble now,' thought Tommy.

At that moment a door was pushed open. Appledore came in and set a candle on the ground and a tray on which was a jug of water, a glass, and some bread and cheese. He said in a quiet voice, 'I am about to take the gag off. You will then be able to eat and drink. If, however, you make the slightest sound, I will replace it immediately.'

As soon as Tommy's mouth was free, Appledore held the glass to his lips. The water did him the world of good.

He murmured stiffly, 'That's better. I'm not quite so young as I was. Now for the food, Fritz – or is it Franz?'

The man said quietly, 'My name here is Appledore.' He held the slice of bread and cheese up and Tommy ate it hungrily.

After another drink of water, Tommy asked, 'And what's the next part of the programme?'

For an answer, Appledore replaced the gag and went out.

Tommy was left in darkness. Some time later he was awakened from a confused sleep by the sound of the door opening. This time Haydock and Appledore came in together. The gag was removed and the ropes that held his arms were loosened so that he could sit up and stretch his arms.

Haydock had a pistol with him. Tommy, without much inner confidence, began to play his part. He said indignantly, 'Look here, Haydock, what's the meaning of all this? I've been attacked – kidnapped!'

The Commander was shaking his head. He remarked coldly, 'Don't waste your breath. You play your role very well, but it's of no importance to me whether you're a member of the British Intelligence, or merely a clever <u>amateur</u> . . .'

'How dare you . . .'

'That's enough, Meadowes.'

'I tell you . . .'

Haydock thrust his angry face forwards. 'Be quiet, damn you. Earlier on it would have mattered to find out who you were and who sent you. Now it doesn't. The time's short, you see. And you didn't have the chance to report to anyone what you'd found out.'

'The police will be looking for me as soon as I'm reported missing.'

Haydock showed his teeth in a sudden smile. 'I've had the police here. Good men – both friends of mine. They were very concerned about your disappearance, but it's quite clear that you left this house well and alive. They would never dream of looking for you here.'

'You can't keep me here for ever,' Tommy said.

Haydock said, putting on his most British manner, 'It won't be necessary, my dear fellow. Only until tomorrow night. A boat will arrive at my little cove – and we're sending you on a <u>voyage</u> for your health – though I don't think you'll be alive, or even on board, when it arrives at its <u>destination</u>.'

'Why didn't you kill me straight away?'

'It's such hot weather, my dear fellow. Just occasionally our sea communications are interrupted, and if that were to happen – well, in this heat, if there was a delay, a dead body would soon become very obvious.'

'I see,' said Tommy.

He did see. He was to be kept alive until the boat arrived. Then he would be killed and his dead body taken out to sea. Nothing would ever connect his body, when found, with *Smugglers' Rest*.

'I just came along,' continued Haydock, 'to ask whether there is anything we could do for you – afterwards?'

Tommy reflected. Then he said, 'Thanks – but I won't ask you to take a <u>lock of</u> my <u>hair</u> to my wife or anything of that kind. She'll only miss me when I stop paying the bills – but I dare say she'll soon find a friend elsewhere.'

He felt he must create the impression that he was operating alone. If no one became suspicious of Tuppence, then the game might still be won.

'As you please,' said Haydock. 'If you did wish to send a message to – your friend – we would see that it was delivered.'

So he was anxious to get a little information. Tommy shook his head.

'Nothing. No message.'

'Very well.' Haydock nodded to Appledore. The latter replaced the ropes and the gag. The two men went out, locking the door behind them.

Tommy felt anything but cheerful. He faced a rapidly approaching death with no means of leaving any clue behind him about the information he had discovered. His body was completely helpless. His brain felt completely inactive.

There was, of course, still Tuppence. But whoever Tuppence might suspect, it would not be Haydock – two <u>witnesses</u> had proved that Tommy had left *Smugglers' Rest* alive and well. Damn it all, if only he had been more on his guard . . .

If only he could get his mouth free, he could shout for help! Somebody might hear through that tiny window high up in one corner of the room, though it was very unlikely.

For the next half-hour he tried to loosen the ropes that they had tied him up with, and bite through the gag. It was all hopeless, however. Haydock and Appledore knew their business.

It was, he judged, late afternoon. Haydock, he guessed, had gone out; he had heard no sounds from overhead. He was probably playing golf, discussing with his friends at the clubhouse the mystery of what had happened to Meadowes!

'He dined with me that night and seemed quite normal. Then he just <u>disappeared into the blue</u>.'

Tommy <u>groaned</u> with <u>fury</u>. That cheerful English manner! It was wonderful what a first-class actor could convince people of. So here he was, a complete failure, tied up like a chicken.

What was that?

He strained his ears listening to a far-off sound. Only some man singing a song. And here *he* was, unable to make a sound to attract anyone's attention. The singing came nearer. A most untuneful noise. But the song was recognisable. It dated from the last war – and had been revived for this one.

'If you were the only girl in the world and I was the only boy.'

How often he had sung that in 1917 – but this fellow simply couldn't sing in tune! Suddenly Tommy's body grew tense. Surely there was only one person who always went wrong in that particular way!

'Albert!' thought Tommy.

Albert, <u>prowling</u> round *Smugglers' Rest*. And here he was, unable to move hand or foot, unable to make a sound . . . Wait a minute. Was he? There was just one sound – not so easy with the mouth shut as with the mouth open, but it could be done.

Desperately Tommy began to <u>snore</u>. He snored and snored – short snore, short snore, short snore – pause – long snore, long snore, long snore – pause – short snore, short snore, short snore . . .

Tommy was snoring the <u>Morse Code</u>.

'Dot, dot, dot, dash, dash, dash, dot, dot, dot.'

SOS – the international signal that someone needed help.

Chapter 12

Although Tuppence went to bed in an <u>optimistic</u> mood, she suffered a severe reaction in those early morning hours when human hope sinks to its lowest. On going down to breakfast, however, her spirits rose with the sight of a letter sitting on her plate addressed in awkward handwriting. Tuppence opened the letter.

'Dear Patricia,

Auntie Grace is, I am afraid, much worse today. The doctors do not actually say she is dying, but I am afraid that there cannot be much hope. If you want to see her before the end, I think you should come today. If you take the 10.20 train to Yarrow, a friend will meet you with his car.

Look forward to seeing you again, dear, in spite of the sad reason.

Yours ever,
Penelope Playne.'

It was all Tuppence could do to control her joy. Good old Penny Plain!

After breakfast, Tuppence rang up the dressmaker's and cancelled a fitting for a coat and skirt for that afternoon. She then went to see Mrs Perenna and explained that she might be away from home for a night or two.

She went up to her room to get ready. Betty Sprot came running out of the Cayleys' bedroom with a <u>mischievous</u> smile on her face.

'What have you been doing?' demanded Tuppence.

Betty gurgled, 'Goosey, goosey gander . . .'

Tuppence chanted, 'Whither will you wander? Upstairs!' She lifted Betty high over her head. 'Downstairs!' She rolled her on the floor.

At this minute Mrs Sprot appeared and Betty was taken off to be dressed for her walk.

'Hide?' said Betty hopefully. 'Hide?'

'You can't play hide-and-seek now,' said Mrs Sprot.

It was ten o'clock as she left *Sans Souci*. She had plenty of time. She looked up at the sky, and in doing so stepped into a dark puddle by the gatepost. Without apparently noticing it, she went on. Her heart was dancing. Success – success – they were going to succeed.

★ ★ ★

Yarrow was a small country station where the village was some distance from the railway. A car was waiting outside the station. A good-looking young man was driving it. He touched two fingers to his cap to Tuppence, but the gesture of respect didn't seem to be one he was used to making. Tuppence kicked the front tyre.

'Isn't this rather flat?'

'We haven't got far to go, Madam.'

She nodded and got into the car. They drove not towards the village but towards the hills. After taking a winding road over a hill, they took a side-track that went down sharply into a deep valley. From the shadow of a small group of trees, a man stepped out to meet them.

The car stopped and Tuppence, getting out, went to meet Anthony Marsdon.

'Beresford's all right,' he said quickly. 'We located him yesterday. He's a prisoner – the Fifth Columnists captured him – and for good reasons he's staying where he is for another twelve hours. You see, there's a small boat due in at a certain place – and we really want to catch it. That's why Beresford's not escaping – we don't want them to realise that we know what they're up to until the last minute.' He looked at her anxiously. 'You do understand, don't you?'

'Oh, yes!' Tuppence was staring at a strange mass of material that was half-hidden by the trees.

'He'll be absolutely all right,' continued the young man seriously.

'Of course Tommy will be all right,' said Tuppence impatiently. 'You needn't talk to me as though I was a child of two. We're both ready to run a few risks. What's that thing over there?'

'Well . . .' The young man hesitated. 'That's just it. I've been ordered to put a certain <u>proposal</u> before you. But – but well, frankly, I don't like doing it. You see . . .'

Tuppence gave him a cold look. 'Why don't you like doing it?'

'Well – you're Deborah's mother. And I mean – what would Deb say to me if – if . . .'

'If I were killed?' inquired Tuppence. 'Personally, if I were you, I wouldn't mention it to her. Just tell me about the dangerous and unpleasant job I have to do.'

'You know,' said the young man with enthusiasm, 'I think you're splendid, simply splendid.'

'Enough compliments,' said Tuppence. 'I'm admiring myself a good deal, so there's no need for you to join in. What exactly is the big idea?'

Tony pointed to the material in the trees 'That,' he said, 'is a <u>parachute</u>.'

'Aha,' said Tuppence. Her eyes shone.

'There was just one parachutist,' went on Marsdon. 'Fortunately the <u>LDV</u>s around here are an alert group of men. The parachutist was seen and they captured her.'

'Her?'

'Yes, her! A woman dressed as a hospital nurse. Medium height, middle-aged, with dark hair and with a slim figure.'

'In fact', said Tuppence, 'a woman not unlike me?'

'Exactly,' said Tony. 'The next part of it is up to you.'

Tuppence smiled. She said, 'Where do I go and what do I do?'

'I say, Mrs Beresford, what magnificent courage you've got.'

'Where do I go and what do I do?' repeated Tuppence impatiently.

'We don't have much information, unfortunately. In the woman's pocket there was a piece of paper with these words on it in German. "Walk to Leatherbarrow – due east from the stone cross. 14 St Asalph's Rd. Dr Binion."'

Tuppence looked up. On the hilltop nearby was a stone cross.

'That's it,' said Tony. 'All the signposts have been removed, of course, in case they helped the enemy. But Leatherbarrow's quite a big place, and walking due east from the cross you're sure to find it.'

'How far?'

'Five miles.'

Tuppence grinned. 'Healthy walking exercise,' she said. 'I hope Dr Binion offers me lunch when I get there.'

'Do you know German, Mrs Beresford?'

'Just a few tourist phrases. I will have to be firm about speaking English – and say my instructions were to do so. Well, lead me to it.'

'We've got everything here – and a policewoman who's an expert in the art of make-up,' explained Tony.

Just inside the trees there was a <u>shed</u>. At the door was a competent-looking middle-aged woman. She looked at Tuppence and nodded approvingly. Inside the shed, seated on an old box, they put on Tuppence's make-up. Finally the policewoman stood back and remarked, 'There, now, I think we've made a very nice job of it. What do you think, sir?'

'Very good indeed,' said Tony.

Tuppence stretched out her hand and took the mirror the other woman was holding. She looked at her own face seriously and could hardly hold back a cry of surprise.

Her eyebrows had been trimmed to an entirely different shape, which changed her whole expression. Her hair, pulled forward over her ears, hid small pieces of <u>sticking plaster</u> that tightened the skin of her face and altered its shape. Skilful make-up had added several years to her age, with heavy lines running down each side of the mouth. Her whole face now had a rather foolish look to it.

'It's very clever,' said Tuppence admiringly.

The other woman produced two slices of thin rubber. 'Do you think you could manage to wear these in your cheeks?'

Tuppence slipped them in and moved her mouth carefully.

'It's not really too uncomfortable.'

Tony then left the shed and Tuppence took off her own clothing and put on the nurse's uniform. It fitted quite well. The dark blue hat added the final touch to her new personality. She rejected, however, the heavy square-toed shoes.

'If I've got to walk five miles,' she said, 'it's much better if I do it in my own shoes.'

Both Tony and the policewoman agreed that this was sensible – particularly as Tuppence's own shoes were dark blue ones that went well with the uniform. She looked with interest into the dark blue handbag – face powder; lipstick; two pounds fourteen and sixpence in English money; a handkerchief and an identity card in the name of Freda Elton, 4 Manchester Road, Sheffield. Tuppence exchanged her own powder and lipstick for the ones in the bag and stood up, prepared to set out.

Tony Marsdon turned his head away. He said abruptly, 'I feel very bad about letting you do this.'

'I know just how you feel.'

'But, you see, it's absolutely vital that we should get some idea of just where and how the attack will come.'

Tuppence patted him on the arm. 'Don't you worry, my child. Believe it or not, I'm enjoying myself!'

★ ★ ★

Rather tired, Tuppence stood outside 14 St Asalph's Road and saw that Dr Binion was a dental surgeon and not a doctor. From the corner of her eye she saw Tony Marsdon. He was sitting in a fast-looking car outside a house farther down the street. It had been thought necessary for Tuppence to walk to Leatherbarrow exactly as instructed. Tony, with the policewoman, had taken a different route before approaching Leatherbarrow. Everything was now ready.

Tuppence crossed the road and rang the bell. The door was opened by an elderly woman.

'Dr Binion?' said Tuppence.

The woman looked her slowly up and down. 'You will be Nurse Elton, I suppose.'

'Yes.'

'Then you will come up to the doctor's surgery.'

She stood back and the door closed behind Tuppence, who found herself standing in a narrow hall. The maid went up the stairs in front of her and opened a door on the first floor.

'Please wait. The doctor will come to you.'

She went out, shutting the door behind her. A very ordinary dentist's surgery – somewhat old and worn out. Soon the door would open and 'Dr Binion' would come in. Who would Dr Binion be? A stranger? Or someone she had seen before? If it was the person she was half expecting to see . . .

The door opened. The man who entered was not at all the person Tuppence had thought she might see! It was someone she had never considered as being N.

It was Commander Haydock.

Chapter 13

Would the Commander recognise her? Tuppence had so prepared herself before this meeting to show no recognition or surprise, no matter whom she might see. She felt reasonably sure that she had showed no signs of surprise when she recognised Haydock. She rose to her feet and stood there, standing in a respectful attitude.

'So you have arrived,' said the Commander.

He spoke in English and his manner was exactly the same as usual.

'Yes,' said Tuppence, 'Nurse Elton.'

Haydock smiled as though at a joke. 'Nurse Elton! Excellent.' He looked at her approvingly. 'You look absolutely right. And do you know what you have to do? Sit down, please.'

Tuppence sat down obediently. She replied, 'I was told to take detailed instructions from you.'

'Very proper,' said Haydock. There was a faint suggestion of amusement in his voice. 'Do you know the day?'

'The fourth.'

Haydock looked surprised. A heavy frown deepened the lines in his <u>forehead</u>. 'So you know that, do you?' he muttered. He paused for a minute, and then asked, 'You have heard, no doubt, of *Sans Souci*?'

'No,' said Tuppence firmly.

There was a strange smile on the Commander's face.

'That surprises me very much – since you have been living there for the last month.'

There was dead silence. The Commander said, 'What about that, Mrs Blenkensop?'

'I don't know what you mean, Dr Binion. I landed by parachute this morning.'

Again Haydock smiled – definitely an unpleasant smile. He continued, 'A few yards of material pushed into a bush create a wonderful <u>illusion</u>, Mrs Blenkensop! Or perhaps you would prefer me to address you by your real name of Beresford?'

Again there was a silence. Tuppence took a deep breath.

Haydock nodded. 'You've lost the game.'

There was a faint click and the blue steel of a pistol showed in his hand. His voice took on a <u>grim</u> note as he added, 'And I should advise you not to make any noise. You'd be dead before you made so much as a single cry, and even if you did manage to scream, it wouldn't get you any attention. Patients who are under anaesthetic often cry out, you know.'

Tuppence said quietly, 'You seem to have thought of everything. Has it occurred to you that I have friends who know where I am?'

'Ah! You are thinking of young Marsdon. I'm sorry, Mrs Beresford, but Anthony happens to be one of our most enthusiastic supporters in this country. As I said just now, a few yards of material creates a wonderful effect. You believed the parachute idea quite easily.'

'I don't see the point of all this acting!'

'Don't you? We don't want your friends to find you too easily. If they pick up your trail, it will lead to Yarrow and to a man in a car. The fact that a hospital nurse, of quite different appearance, walked into Leatherbarrow between one and two o'clock will hardly be connected with your disappearance.'

'Very clever,' said Tuppence.

Haydock said, 'I admire your courage, you know. I admire it very much. I'm sorry to have to force you – but it's vital that we should know just exactly how much you discovered at *Sans Souci*.'

Tuppence did not answer.

Haydock said quietly, 'I'd advise you to tell me everything. There are certain – possibilities – in a dentist's chair and these instruments can cause a lot of damage.'

Tuppence gave him an arrogant look.

'Yes,' Haydock observed slowly, 'I imagine you've got a lot of courage. But what about the other half of the picture?'

'What do you mean?'

'I'm talking about Thomas Beresford, your husband, who has lately been living at *Sans Souci* under the name of Mr Meadowes, and who is now very conveniently tied up in the cellar of my house.'

Tuppence declared, 'I don't believe it.'

'Because of the Penny Plain letter? Don't you realise that that was just a clever bit of work on the part of young Anthony. You fell into his <u>trap</u> nicely when you gave him the code.'

Tuppence's voice trembled. 'Then Tommy – then Tommy –'

'Tommy', said Commander Haydock, 'is where he has been all along – completely in my power! It's up to you now. If you answer my questions satisfactorily, there's a chance for him. If you don't – well, he'll be knocked on the head, taken out to sea and thrown overboard.'

Tuppence was silent for a minute or two – then she asked, 'What do you want to know?'

'I want to know who employed you, what your means of communication with that person or persons are, what you have reported so far, and exactly what you know?'

Tuppence shrugged her shoulders. 'I could tell you what lies I choose,' she pointed out.

'No, because I will proceed to test what you say.' He drew his chair a little nearer. 'My dear woman – I know just what you feel about it all, but believe me when I say I really do admire both you and your husband immensely. You've got strength and bravery. It's people like you that will be needed in the new State – the State that will arise in this country when your present weak government is destroyed. We want to turn some of our enemies into friends – those that are worthwhile. If I have to give the order that ends your husband's life, I will do it – it's my duty – but I will feel really bad about having to do so! He's a fine fellow.

Let me explain what so few people in this country seem to understand. Our Leader does not intend to conquer this country. He intends to create a new Britain – a Britain strong in its own power – ruled, not by Germans, but by Englishmen. And the best type of Englishmen – Englishmen with brains and education and courage. A brave new world, as Shakespeare puts it.

'We want no more confusion and inefficiency. And in this new state we want people like you and your husband – brave and intelligent enemies – to be our friends. You would be surprised if you knew how many there are in this country, as there are in other countries, who have sympathy with us and believe in our aims. Between us all we will create a new Europe – a Europe of peace and progress. Try and see it that way – because, I assure you – it is that way . . .'

His voice was <u>mesmerizing</u> and he looked the perfect picture of an honest British sailor.

Tuppence stared at him and searched her mind for an appropriate phrase. She was only able to find one that was both childish and rude. 'Goosey, goosey gander!' said Tuppence, reciting the <u>nursery rhyme</u> she had last repeated while playing with Betty.

★ ★ ★

The effect on Haydock was so intense that she was quite amazed. He jumped to his feet, his face went dark purple with anger, and in a second all resemblance to a cheerful British sailor had vanished. She saw what Tommy had once seen – an angry Prussian officer. He swore at her fluently in German. Then, changing to English, he shouted, 'You dangerous little fool! Don't you realise you give yourself away completely answering like that? You can't be allowed to live now – you and your precious husband.'

Raising his voice he called, 'Anna!'

The woman came into the room. Haydock pushed the pistol into her hand. 'Watch her. Shoot if necessary.'

He went out of the room. Tuppence looked at Anna, who stood in front of her with an expressionless face. 'Would you really shoot me?'

Anna answered quietly, 'In the last war my son was killed, my Otto. I was thirty-eight, then – I am sixty-two now – but I have not forgotten.'

Tuppence looked at the broad face. It reminded her of the Polish woman, Vanda Polonska. She had that same frightening determination.

Something came to Tuppence's brain – some vague memory. Something that she had always tried to remember. Something that she had known but had never succeeded in bringing into focus in her mind.

The door opened. Commander Haydock came back into the room. He shouted out, still very angry, 'Where is it? Where have you hidden it?'

Tuppence stared at him. What he was saying did not make sense to her. She had taken nothing and hidden nothing. Haydock said to Anna, 'Get out.'

The woman handed the pistol to him and left the room at once. Haydock threw himself into a chair and seemed to be trying hard to control himself. He said, 'You can't escape, you know. I've got you – and I've got ways of making people speak – not pretty ways. You'll have to tell the truth in the end. Now then, what have you done with it?'

Tuppence was quick to see that here, at least, was something that gave her the possibility of bargaining. If only she could work out what it was she was supposed to have in her possession!

She said cautiously, 'How do you know I've got it?'

'From what you said, you silly little fool. You haven't got it on you – that we know, since you changed completely into this nurse's uniform.'

'Suppose I posted it to someone?' said Tuppence.

'Don't be an idiot. Everything you posted since yesterday has been examined. You didn't post it. No, there's only one thing you could have done – hidden it in *Sans Souci* before you left this morning. I give you just three minutes to tell me where that hiding-place is.'

He put his watch down on the table. 'Three minutes, Mrs Thomas Beresford.'

The clock above the fireplace ticked. Tuppence sat quite still with a blank expressionless face. It didn't show the thoughts racing behind it. In a flash of understanding she saw everything – and realised at last who was the centre of the whole organisation.

It came as quite a shock to her when Haydock said, 'Ten seconds more . . .'

As if in a dream she watched him, saw the arm holding the pistol rise, heard him count.

'One, two, three, four, five . . .'

He had reached eight when the shot rang out and he collapsed forward on his chair, a puzzled expression on his broad red face. He had been so focussed on watching his <u>victim</u> that he had been unaware of the door behind him opening.

In a flash Tuppence was on her feet. She pushed her way past the uniformed men in the doorway, and took hold urgently of an arm belonging to someone she knew. 'Mr Grant!'

'Yes, yes, my dear, it's all right now – you've been wonderful . . .'

Tuppence ignored these reassurances. 'Quick! There's no time to lose. You've got a car here?'

'Yes.' He stared at her.

'A fast one? We must get to *Sans Souci* at once. If only we're in time. Before they telephone here, and get no answer.'

Two minutes later they were in the car and it was making its way through the streets of Leatherbarrow. Then they were out in the open country, moving fast.

Mr Grant asked no questions. He was content to sit quietly whilst Tuppence watched the speedometer in an agony of fear. The driver had been given his orders and he drove with all the speed the car was capable of.

Tuppence only spoke once. 'Tommy?'

'He's quite all right. He was rescued half an hour ago.'

She nodded. Now, at last, they were nearing Leahampton. The car raced and twisted through the town, then up the hill. Tuppence jumped out and she and Mr Grant ran up the drive. The hall door, as usual, was open. There was no one in sight. Tuppence ran lightly up the stairs. She glanced inside her own room as she passed it, and noted the open drawers and untidy bed. She nodded to herself and passed on, along the upper hall and into the room occupied by Mr and Mrs Cayley.

The room was empty. It looked peaceful and smelt slightly of medicines. Tuppence ran across to the bed and pulled at the coverings. They fell to the ground and Tuppence put her hand under the mattress. She turned triumphantly to Mr Grant with a well-worn child's picture-book in her hand.

'Here you are. It's all in here!'

'What on earth . . .?'

They turned. Mrs Sprot was standing in the doorway staring at them.

'And now,' said Tuppence, 'let me introduce you to M! Yes. Mrs Sprot! I should have known all along.'

It was left to Mrs Cayley, arriving in the doorway a moment later, to introduce the appropriate anti-climax.

'Oh dear,' said Mrs Cayley, looking with dismay at her husband's bed. 'Whatever will Mr Cayley say?'

Chapter 14

'I should have known it all along,' exclaimed Tuppence.

She was calming her nerves with a large glass of brandy, and was smiling broadly at Tommy and Mr Grant and Albert, who was sitting with a pint of beer and grinning from ear to ear.

'Tell us about it, Tuppence,' urged Tommy.

'You first,' said Tuppence.

'There's not much for me to tell,' said Tommy. 'A complete accident in Haydock's bathroom led me to the secret wireless transmitter. I tried to pretend I thought it must have belonged to Hahn, the previous owner of *Smugglers'*, but Haydock was too clever for me.'

Tuppence nodded and said, 'He telephoned Mrs Sprot at once. And she ran out into the drive and waited for you.'

'After that,' said Tommy, 'the <u>credit</u> belongs entirely to Albert. He was investigating around Haydock's place because it was the last place I'd been. I did some intense morse-code snoring and he understood it immediately. He went off to Mr Grant with the news and the two of them came back late that night. I did some more snoring! The result was that I agreed to remain in the cellar so that we could catch the people in the boat when it arrived.'

Mr Grant added his part of the story, 'When Haydock went off this morning, our people took charge at *Smugglers' Rest*. We captured the boat this evening.'

'And now, Tuppence,' said Tommy. 'Your story.'

'Well, to begin with, I was the biggest fool all along! I suspected everybody here *except* Mrs Sprot! Then Tommy disappeared. I was just getting a plan together with Albert when suddenly Anthony Marsdon arrived. He seemed all right to begin with – he was the usual sort of young man that Deborah often has around. But two things made me think a bit. First, I became more and more convinced as I talked to him that I had never seen him before and that he had never been to the flat. The second thing was that, though he seemed to know all about *my* working at Leahampton, he assumed that Tommy was in Scotland. Now, that seemed all wrong. If he knew about anyone, it would be Tommy since I wasn't here officially. That seemed very strange to me.

'Mr Grant had told me that Fifth Columnists were everywhere. So why shouldn't one of them be working in Deborah's department? I was suspicious enough to lay a trap for him. I told him that Tommy and I had fixed up a code for communicating with each other. I told Anthony we used the saying *Penny plain, tuppence coloured* in letters and said we spelt plain as Playne.

'As I hoped, he believed it completely! I got a letter this morning, which gave him away totally. I'd worked out all the arrangements with Albert beforehand. All I had to do was to pretend to be ringing up a dressmaker to cancel a fitting but really I was phoning Albert to let him know that Anthony was a traitor and that N or M, or both of them, wanted to know more about me and what I knew.'

'It gave me a shock,' said Albert. 'I drove up with a baker's van and we poured a pool of aniseed just outside the gate.'

'And then . . .' Tuppence took up the story, 'I came out and walked in the aniseed. Of course it was easy for the baker's van to follow me to the station and then someone else, who was also following me, came up behind me and heard me book a ticket to Yarrow. It was after that that it might have been difficult.'

'The dogs we'd brought followed the smell of the aniseed well,' said Mr Grant. 'They picked it up at Yarrow station and again on the track the tyre had made after you kicked your shoe on it. It led us down to the trees and up again to the stone cross and where you had walked over the hills. The enemy had no idea we could follow you easily after they had seen you set off walking and had driven off themselves.'

'All the same,' said Albert, 'it made me very worried, knowing you were in that house and not knowing what might be happening to you there. We got in a back window and caught the foreign woman as she came down the stairs. We came in just in time to save you.'

'I knew you'd come,' said Tuppence. 'The thing was for me to keep things going as long as I could. What was really exciting was the way I suddenly saw the whole thing and what a fool I'd been.'

'How did you see it?' asked Tommy.

'Goosey, goosey, gander,' said Tuppence promptly. 'When I said that to Commander Haydock he went absolutely mad. And not just because it was silly and rude. No, I saw at once that it meant something to him. And then there was the expression on that German woman's face – Anna – it was like the Polish woman's, and then, of course, I thought of King Solomon, who ruled Israel thousands of years ago, and I saw the whole thing.'

Tommy gave a sigh of <u>exasperation</u>. 'Tuppence, if you say that once again, I'll shoot you myself. Saw all what? And what on earth has Solomon got to do with it?'

'Do you remember that two women came to Solomon with a baby and both said it was hers, but Solomon said, "Very well, cut it in two." And the false mother said, "All right." But the real mother said, "No, let the other woman have it." You see, the real mother couldn't face her child being killed. Well, the night that Mrs Sprot shot the other woman, you all said what a miracle it was and how easily she might have shot the child. Of course, it ought to have been quite clear then! If it *had* been her child, she wouldn't have risked that shot for a minute. It proved that Betty wasn't her child. And that's why she absolutely had to shoot the other woman.'

'Why?'

'Because, of course, the other woman was the child's real mother.' Tuppence's voice shook a little. 'Poor thing – poor hunted thing. She came over to England as a refugee, with nothing, and so she was grateful when Mrs Sprot asked if she could <u>adopt</u> her baby and gave her money.'

'But why did Mrs Sprot want to adopt the child?'

'<u>Camouflage</u>! It would be hard to believe that a master spy would involve her child in the business. That's the main reason why I never considered Mrs Sprot seriously. Simply because of the child. But Betty's real mother had a terrible <u>longing</u> for her baby and she found out where Mrs Sprot was living and came down here. She waited around for her chance, and at last she got it and went off with the child.

'Mrs Sprot, of course, was terribly worried. At all costs she didn't want the police to get involved. So she wrote that message and pretended she'd found it in her bedroom, and she made sure Commander Haydock was brought in to help. Then, when we'd tracked down the poor woman, Mrs Sprot couldn't risk being discovered, so she shot her. She pretended not to know anything about <u>firearms</u> when, in fact, she was a very fine shot! Yes, she killed that poor woman – and because of that, I've no pity for her. She was bad through and through.'

Tuppence paused, then she went on, 'Another thing that ought to have given me a hint was the likeness between Vanda Polonska and Betty. It was Betty the woman reminded me of all along. And then the child's strange play with my shoelaces. How much more likely that she'd seen her "mother" do that – not Carl von Deinim! But as soon as Mrs Sprot saw what the child was doing, she placed a lot of evidence for us to find in Carl's room and added the master touch of a shoelace soaked in secret ink.'

'I'm glad that Carl wasn't involved,' said Tommy. 'I liked him.'

'He's not been shot, has he?' asked Tuppence anxiously, noting the past tense.

Mr Grant shook his head. 'He's all right,' he grinned. 'As a matter of fact I've got a little surprise for you there.'

Tuppence's face lit up as she said, 'I'm terribly glad – for Sheila's sake! Of course we were idiots to suspect Mrs Perenna.'

'She was mixed up in some IRA activities, nothing more,' said Mr Grant.

'I suspected Mrs O'Rourke a little – and sometimes the Cayleys . . .'

'And I suspected Bletchley,' put in Tommy.

'And all the time', said Tuppence, 'it was that silly creature we just thought of as "Betty's mother".'

'Not exactly silly,' said Mr Grant. 'A very dangerous woman and a very clever actress. And, I'm sorry to say, English by birth.'

Tuppence said, 'Then I've no pity or admiration for her – it wasn't even her own country she was working for.' She looked at Mr Grant. 'Did you find what you wanted?'

Mr Grant nodded. 'It was all in that old collection of children's books.'

'The ones that Betty said were "nasty"!' Tuppence exclaimed.

'They *were* nasty,' said Mr Grant dryly. '*Little Jack Horner* contained very full details of our naval operations. *Johnny Head in Air* did the same for the Air Force. Details of the Army were appropriately hidden in *There Was a Little Man and He Had a Little Gun*.'

'And *Goosey, Goosey, Gander*?' asked Tuppence.

Mr Grant said, 'That book contains, written in invisible ink, a full list of all the important people who have agreed to assist in an invasion of this country. Among them were two chief constables, an air vice-marshal, two generals, the head of an armaments works, a cabinet minister, many police superintendents, commanders of local volunteer defence organizations, and various military and naval junior officers, as well as members of our own Intelligence Force.'

Tommy and Tuppence stared at him.

'Incredible!' said Tommy.

Grant shook his head. 'You don't understand the force of the German propaganda. It appeals to something in a man, some desire for power. These people were ready to betray their country not for money, but in a kind of superior pride in what they themselves were going to achieve for that country. In every other country it has been the same. And you can see that, with such people able to issue contradictory orders and confuse operations, the invasion would have had every chance of succeeding.'

'And now?' said Tuppence.

Mr Grant smiled. 'And now,' he said, 'let them come! We'll be ready for them!'

Chapter 15

'Darling,' said Deborah, as they sat at a table in the ballroom of the *Ritz Hotel* in London, 'do you know I almost thought the most terrible things about you?'

'Did you?' said Tuppence. 'When?'

Her eyes rested lovingly on her daughter's dark head.

'That time when you went off to Scotland to join Father and I thought you were with Aunt Gracie. I almost thought you were having an affair with someone.'

'Oh, Deb, did you?'

'Not really, of course. Not at *your* age. And of course I knew you and Father are devoted to each other. It was really an idiot called Tony Marsdon who put it into my head. Do you know, Mother, they discovered he was a Fifth Columnist.'

'Did you like him at all?'

'Tony? Oh no – he was always so boring. Oh, I must dance to this tune – I love it.'

She floated away in the arms of a fair-haired young man, smiling up at him sweetly. Tuppence followed their movements for a few minutes, then her eyes looked over to where a tall young man in Air Force uniform was dancing with a slim, fair-haired girl.

'I do think, Tommy,' said Tuppence, 'that our children are rather nice.'

'Here's Sheila,' said Tommy.

He got up as Sheila Perenna came towards their table. She was dressed in a bright green evening dress which showed up her dark beauty. It was an unhappy beauty tonight and she greeted her host and hostess rather ungraciously.

'I've come, you see,' she said, 'as I promised. But I can't think why you wanted to ask me.'

'We have a nice partner for you to dance with,' said Tommy smiling.

'I don't want to dance.'

'You will like the partner we've asked to meet you,' said Tuppence grinning.

'I . . .' Sheila began. Then stopped, for Carl von Deinim was walking across the floor. 'You!'

'I, myself,' said Carl.

There was something a little different about Carl von Deinim this evening. Sheila stared at him. The colour had come to her cheeks, turning them a deep glowing red. She said breathlessly, 'I thought they would keep you interned?'

Carl shook his head. 'There is no reason to intern me. You have got to forgive me, Sheila, for lying to you. I am not, you see, Carl von Deinim. I took his name for reasons of my own.'

He looked questioningly at Tuppence, who said: 'Go ahead. Tell her.'

'Carl von Deinim was my friend. I knew him in England some years ago. I renewed my friendship with him in Germany just before the war. I was there then on special business for this country.'

'You were in British Intelligence?' asked Sheila.

'Yes. And I had some very near escapes. My plans were known when they should not have been known. I realised that the service had traitors in it. Carl was not a Nazi. He was interested only in his job – a job I myself had also worked at – research chemistry. He decided, shortly before war broke out, to escape to England. His brothers had been sent to concentration camps. There would, he thought, be great difficulties in the way of his own escape, but in an almost miraculous way all these difficulties were resolved rather effortlessly. That fact, when he mentioned it to me, it made me suspicious. Why were the authorities making it so easy for von Deinim to leave Germany? It seemed as though they wanted him in England for some reason. My own position was becoming increasingly dangerous. Carl's <u>lodgings</u> were in the same house as mine and one day I found him, to my great sadness, lying dead on his bed. He had become <u>depressed</u> and had taken his own life, leaving a letter behind which I read and kept.

'I decided then to pretend to be Carl. I wanted to get out of Germany – and I also wanted to know why Carl was being encouraged to do so. I dressed his body in my clothes and laid it on my bed. His face was disfigured by the shot he had fired into his head.

'With Carl von Deinim's papers I travelled to England and went to the address to which he had been recommended to go. The address was *Sans Souci*. While I was there I played the part of Carl von Deinim. At first I thought that I should be made to work for the Nazis. I realised later that the part for which my poor friend had been chosen was that of <u>scapegoat</u>.

'When I was arrested on false evidence, I said nothing. I wanted to reveal my own identity as late as possible. I wanted to see what would happen.'

'You should have told me,' Sheila complained.

He said gently, 'If you feel like that – I am sorry.'

His eyes looked into hers. She looked at him angrily and proudly – then the anger melted. 'I suppose you had to do what you did . . .'

'Darling, come and dance.' They moved off together.

Tuppence sighed. 'Why did he search my room that day? That led us in completely the wrong direction.'

Tommy gave a laugh. 'I believe he thought Mrs Blenkensop wasn't a very convincing person. In fact – while we were suspecting him, he was suspecting us.'

'Hello, you two,' said Derek Beresford as he and his partner danced past his parents' table. 'Why don't you come and dance?' He smiled encouragingly at them.

'They are so kind to us, bless them,' said Tuppence, praying to herself, 'Oh keep them safe – don't let anything happen to them . . .'

She looked up to meet Tommy's eyes. He said, 'About that child – will we?'

'Betty? Oh, Tommy, I'm glad you've thought of it, too! I thought it was just me being motherly. You really mean it?'

'That we should adopt her? Why not? She's had a very bad start in life, and it will be fun for us to have someone young growing up with us.'

'Oh Tommy!'

She stretched out her hand and squeezed his. They looked at each other.

'We always do want the same things,' said Tuppence happily.

Deborah, passing Derek on the floor, murmured to him, 'Just look at those two – actually holding hands! They're rather sweet, aren't they? Poor things – they are having such a boring time in this war. I think we really must try to put more fun and excitement into their lives . . .'

Character list

Tommy (Thomas) Beresford/Mr Meadowes: a middle-aged man who was in British Intelligence in the Great War

Tuppence Beresford/Mrs Blenkensop: Tommy's wife – she was also in British Intelligence

Deborah Beresford: the Beresfords' daughter, who works in the coding department of British Intelligence

Mr Carter/Lord Easthampton: was in charge of British Intelligence but has now retired

Mr Grant: a member of British Intelligence

Mrs Perenna: owner of a boarding house called *Sans Souci*

Mrs O'Rourke: a guest from Ireland at *Sans Souci*

Major Bletchley: a former army officer, he is also a guest at *Sans Souci*

Carl von Deinim: a refugee from Germany

Miss Minton: an elderly unmarried lady, a guest at *Sans Souci*

Mr Cayley: a middle-aged invalid staying at *Sans Souci*

Mrs Cayley: married to Mr Cayley

Mrs Sprot: a young mother staying at *Sans Souci*

Betty Sprot: daughter of Mrs Sprot

Sheila Perenna: Mrs Perenna's daughter

Commander Haydock: a retired Royal Naval officer who lives near *Sans Souci*

Appledore: Commander Haydock's manservant

Albert: now the owner of a pub, Albert once worked for the Beresfords

Tony Marsdon: a colleague of Deborah's

Derek Beresford: Deborah's brother – a pilot in the Royal Air Force

Mrs Rowley: Deborah's landlady

Gladys: Mrs Rowley's maid

Anna: a low-ranking German spy

Cultural notes

World War II (1939 to 1945)

The war began with the invasion of Poland by Nazi Germany on September 1, 1939. Great Britain, which had treaties with Poland, declared war on Germany when it refused to withdraw from Poland. *N or M?* is set in 1940. This was the year that Germany invaded France, Belgium, the Netherlands and Luxembourg. British troops – known as the British Expeditionary Force (BEF) – had been sent to Europe and were poorly equipped and outnumbered by German soldiers. They had to move back towards the French port of Dunkirk, where most British soldiers were rescued in hundreds of small boats.

Nazi

This is short for the name of the National Socialist movement formed in Germany after World War I. In 1933 Adolf Hitler became the 'Leader' (referred to by Haydock in the story) – the Leader is called the *Führer* in German.

Blitzkrieg

In German, this means 'lightning war' and it describes the method the German military used to invade other countries during World War II. While cities and military air bases were bombed from the air and heavy guns attacked border areas, tanks moved quickly to break through the enemy's lines of defence. Infantry units, i.e. soldiers on foot, followed them closely. At all times the Germans would move forward very quickly, making it impossible for defending forces to respond effectively.

Evacuees

Children were sent away to the countryside because people were afraid that Germany would bomb Britain's major cities. In some cases the mother accompanied the children, but the majority were sent alone and were taken in by strangers. In the story, the fear of bombing is mentioned as the reason why Mrs Sprot moved to the guesthouse *Sans Souci* with her young child while her husband stayed in London.

Home defence

Winston Churchill, who became Britain's prime minister during the war, had asked for a home defence force to be formed in 1939, but it wasn't until May 1940 that men between the ages of 17 and 65 were asked to volunteer for the unpaid LDV (Local Defence Volunteers). By July 1.5 million men had come forward and social groups, such as golf club members, formed their own units, which the press called 'the parashots'. Men who had been officers in World War I often led these units. In the story Commander Haydock is also an Air Raid Protection warden. The ARP was responsible for ensuring no lights were on during the night, so that enemy pilots could not see the location of towns and cities.

In July, the LDV was renamed as the 'Home Guard' and their duty, if Britain was invaded, was to delay and obstruct the Germans by any means. They were organized into sections like the regular army. They operated observation posts to watch for any enemy planes and arranged to use church bells to call in all members.

One responsibility was to make it difficult for any enemy arriving in Britain to find their way around. In the story Tony Marsdon mentions that all signposts pointing to towns and villages had been removed, in order to confuse the enemy if they arrived in Britain.

Fifth Column

This term originated during the Spanish Civil War in 1936 when a Nationalist General announced on the radio that the four columns of his forces outside the city of Madrid would be supported by a 'fifth column', a secret army, *inside* the city. Their role was to weaken the government from within. The fear of a fifth column in Britain was widespread in the early stages of the war, with the belief that Germans who lived in Britain were possibly spies, and that Britons who believed in Hitler's cause were working to weaken the country's defences.

For this reason, foreign nationals, especially Germans, were 'interned', i.e. they were put in special camps and kept virtually as prisoners.

Censorship
As part of her role as Mrs Beresford, Tuppence invents three sons who she says are serving in the armed forces. She pretends to exchange information with her sons about where they are fighting, in order to make the spy reveal him or herself. Including information about troop movements in letters was not permitted during the war. Letters to and from soldiers and their families were therefore censored – i.e. they were checked and any information that could be valuable to the enemy was deleted.

Concentration camp
Carl von Deinim mentions that his family members were in concentration camps. These concentration camps were used by the Nazis to imprison Jews and other racial and social groups, before and during World War II. Millions of people were killed in these camps during the war.

Nurse Edith Cavell
Edith Louisa Cavell was a British nurse working in Belgium during World War I. She saved the lives of soldiers from both sides, and helped around 200 British soldiers escape from German-occupied Belgium. She was arrested in Brussels by the Germans and found guilty of treason. She was sentenced to death and shot in 1915.

Her strong religious beliefs required her to help all those who needed it, both German and British soldiers. She was quoted as saying, 'I can't stop while there are lives to be saved'. She is well-known for her statement that 'patriotism is not enough'. It is this that makes Sheila Perenna angry during the conversation about spies.

British military ranks – officers

Army (junior to senior ranks): Second Lieutenant, Lieutenant, Captain, Major, Lieutenant Colonel, Colonel, Brigadier, Major General, Lieutenant General, General, Field Marshal (only in wartime)

Navy (junior to senior ranks): Midshipman, Sub-Lieutenant, Lieutenant, Lieutenant-Commander, Commander, Captain, Commodore, Rear Admiral, Vice Admiral, Admiral, Admiral of the Fleet (only in wartime)

Air Force (junior to senior ranks): Pilot Officer, Flying Officer, Flight Lieutenant, Squadron Leader, Wing Commander, Group Captain, Air Commodore, Air Vice-Marshal, Air Marshal, Air Chief Marshal, Marshal of the Royal Air Force (wartime rank only, honorary in peacetime)

British Intelligence

This refers to the Secret Intelligence Service (SIS) that had been in operation since before World War I. Its main functions were to gather information about potential and real enemies, to run secret agents abroad, to decipher enemy codes, and to carry out secret operations in enemy countries. In the story, Deborah Beresford and Tony Marsdon work in the coding department. They would be responsible for sending and receiving messages to and from agents, using special codes.

IRA

Northern Ireland is part of the United Kingdom. Southern Ireland (Republic of Eire) declared itself neutral at the beginning of World War II. However, the illegal Irish Republican Army (IRA) wanted to free all of Ireland from British rule and had been conducting a bombing campaign on mainland Britain in the six months before the war began.

In the story Sheila Perenna mentions Roger Casement, a man who believed in Irish nationalism. Roger Casement had tried to get German support for Ireland to rebel against Britain during World War I. He was found guilty of treason by the British government and was executed in 1916.

Prussia

Tommy refers to Commander Haydock as behaving and sounding like a Prussian officer. Prussia was an important kingdom in Europe until the mid 20th century. The Prussian military was regarded as extremely well organized and professional, but also aggressive, and brutal in its discipline of its soldiers.

Nursery rhymes

These are songs or poems for young children, often with actions fitted to them to make them more enjoyable and fun. Nursery rhymes are often reproduced in illustrated picture books.

In the story, these rhymes are mentioned: *Goosey Goosey Gander, Little Jack Horner, Johnny Head in Air,* and *There was a Little Man and He had a Little Gun.*

Morse Code

This is the international system of representing letters and numbers, each with a unique number of dots (short signal) and dashes (long signal). It was used for radio communication before voice transmission was possible. In the story, Tommy pretends to snore and uses the most famous morse code message that means 'emergency' – SOS – to signal to Albert. This message consists of 3 short dots for 'S' and 3 long dashes for 'O'. So, 'SOS' is represented by 'dot-dot-dot-dash-dash-dash-dot-dot-dot'.

Glossary

Key

n = noun
v = verb
phr v = phrasal verb
adj = adjective
adv = adverb
excl = exclamation
exp = expression

active service (n)
working in the army, navy or air force

adopt (v)
begin to do something; make someone else's child legally yours

air raid (n)
an attack in which military aircraft drop bombs on people or places

alibi (n)
proof that you were somewhere else when a crime was committed

alliance (n)
a relationship between different countries, political parties, or organizations who work together for some purpose

amateur (n)
someone who does a particular activity as a hobby, not as a job

aniseed (n)
an aromatic plant whose seeds are often used in cooking

anxiety (n)
a feeling of nervousness or worry

Glossary

anxiously (adv)
in a nervous or worried way

arrest (v)
when the police take someone to a police station in order to decide if they should be charged with an offence

assumption (n)
the idea that something is true

authoritative (adj)
powerful and in control

authorities (n)
official organizations with power to make decisions

awkward (adj)
embarrassing and difficult to deal with

balaclava (n)
a close-fitting knitted cap that covers the head, neck and tops of the shoulders often worn by soldiers or mountain climbers

bandage (n)
a long strip of cloth that is tied around a wounded part of someone's body in order to protect or support it

bargain (v)
to discuss what each person will do, pay, or receive

battle (n)
a fight between armies or between groups of ships or planes

betray (v)
to give information to an enemy putting your country or comrades at risk

binoculars (n)
two small telescopes joined together side by side which you look through in order to see things that are far away

blanket (n)
a large piece of thick cloth, especially one which you put on a bed to keep you warm

Blitzkrieg (n)
(see Cultural notes)

bounce (v)
to move up and down

bow (v)
to briefly bend your body towards someone to show respect or to greet them

British Expeditionary Force (n)
British troops sent to Europe during the war

brute (n)
someone who is rough and insensitive

bulldog (n)
a type of dog with a large square head and powerful jaws

bully (n)
a person who uses their strength or power to hurt or frighten you

By Jove (excl)
an old-fashioned expression used to express surprise

(to be) called up (v)
when you are ordered to report for active military service

camouflage (n)
clothing, objects or behaviour which hides what you are really doing

capture (v)
to catch someone or something

cardboard (n)
thick, stiff paper used to make boxes and other containers

Casement
(see Cultural notes)

cave (n)
a large hole in the side of a cliff or hill, or under the ground

cellar (n)
a room underneath a building

censor (n)
a person who has been officially appointed to examine documents and cut out any parts that they consider unacceptable

chant (v)
to repeat the same words over and over again

chase (v)
to run after or follow a person in order to catch them

Chief Constable (n)
a police officer in charge of a large area

cliff (n)
a high area of land with a very steep side, especially next to the sea

clue (n)
something that helps you find the answer to a mystery

clumsy (adj)
moving or handling things in an awkward way

Glossary

code (n)
a system of replacing the words in a message with other words or symbols, so that people who do not know the system cannot understand it

collapse (v)
to suddenly fall down because you are ill or tired

collide (v)
to bump into something or someone

Commander (n)
an officer in charge of a military operation

compliment (v)
to say something nice about someone or something

concentration camp (n)
a prison where non-military prisoners are kept in very bad conditions, usually in wartime

confess (v)
to admit doing something that is wrong or that you are ashamed of

confidential (adj)
spoken or written in secret and should stay secret

contempt (n)
with no respect

contradictory (adj)
two or more facts, ideas, or statements which state or imply that opposite things are true

coroner (n)
the person who is responsible for investigating sudden or unusual deaths

cove (n)
a small bay on the coast

crawl (v)
to move forward on your hands and knees

credit (n)
recognition or praise for doing something good

crop (n)
plants that are grown in large quantities for food

delighted (adj)
extremely pleased and excited about something

depressed (adj)
feeling sad and unable to enjoy anything, because your situation is difficult and unpleasant

destination (n)
the place you are going to

devoted (adj)
caring for or loving something or someone very much

disappear into the blue (exp)
to vanish completely and without explanation

dismay (n)
fear, worry or disappointment

dockyard (n)
an area beside a river or the sea for repairing and loading ships and storing supplies

esplanade (n)
a large, flat open piece of ground, often used for parades

evidence (n)
anything that makes you believe that something is true or exists

exasperation (n)
extreme irritation

eyebrow (n)
the lines of hair which grow above your eyes

eyelash (n)
the hairs which grow on the edges of your eyelids

fellow (n)
a man or a boy

fertiliser (n)
something added to soil or water to make plants more productive

Fifth Column (n)
(see Cultural notes)

firearms (n)
guns

forehead (n)
the flat area at the front of your head above your eyebrows and below where your hair grows

Front (n)
the place where two armies are fighting

frown (v)
to move your eyebrows together because you are annoyed, worried or thinking

fury (n)
very strong anger

fuss (n)
behaviour that is unnecessarily anxious or excited

gadget (n)
a small machine or device which does a useful task

gag (n)
a piece of cloth that is tied round or put inside someone's mouth to stop them from speaking

germ (n)
a very small organism that causes disease

Goosey Goosey Gander
the name of a rhyme for children about a goose

grim (adj)
serious, stern, unattractive, depressing

grin (v)
to smile widely

groan (v)
to make a long low sound of pain, unhappiness, or disapproval

ground (n)
the surface of the earth or the floor of a room

hatred (n)
an extremely strong feeling of dislike

hint (n)
a very small amount of something

host/hostess (n)
the person who has invited the guests and who provides the food, drinks, or entertainment

hysterics (n)
a state of uncontrolled excitement, panic or laughter

ignorance (n)
the state of not knowing something

illusion (n)
something that appears to exist or to be a particular thing but in reality does not exist or is something else

impulse (n)
a sudden desire to do something

inquest (n)
a meeting where evidence is heard about someone's death to find out why they died

Inspector (n)
a police officer who is higher in rank than a sergeant and lower in rank than a superintendent

instinct (n)
the natural tendency that a person has to behave or react in a particular way

Intelligence (n)
the government organization that gathers information about their country's enemies

interfere (v)
to get involved in a situation although it does not concern them and their involvement is not wanted

intern (v)
to put someone in prison for political reasons

invalid (n)
a person who is very ill or disabled and needs to be cared for

invasion (n)
when a foreign army enters a country by force

isolated (adj)
when a place is a long way away from large towns and is difficult to reach

kidnapper (n)
a person who takes someone away illegally and by force, and usually holds them prisoner in order to demand something from their family, employer, or government

knit (v)
to make something from wool using knitting needles

lace (n)
*see **shoelaces**

landlady (n)
a woman who allows you to live or work in a building which she owns, in return for rent

lap (n)
the flat area formed by the top part of your legs when you are sitting down

lay a trap (v)
to trick someone

LDV (n)
Local Defence Volunteer (see Cultural notes: Home defence)

Little Jack Horner
the name of a rhyme for children about a little boy called Jack Horner

lock of hair (n)
a small bunch of hairs on your head that grows in the same direction

longing (n)
a strong desire for someone or something

lodgings (n)
a room in someone's house that is rented

Major (n)
an army officer of medium rank

make an impression (exp)
to have a strong effect on people or a situation

manservant (n)
a man who is employed to work in a house, for example to cook or clean

martyr (n)
someone who is killed or made to suffer greatly because of their religious or political beliefs

matchstick (n)
a short, thin piece of wood used to light a fire

mattress (n)
the comfortable part of a bed which you sleep on

mesmerizing (adj)
fascinating, making it difficult to think about anything else

mischievous (adj)
wanting to have fun by embarrassing people or by playing harmless tricks

Morse Code (n)
a system of transmitting messages as a series of on-off tones, lights or clicks (see Cultural notes)

murmur (v)
to speak very quietly

nasty (adj)
very unpleasant or unattractive

naughty (adj)
behaving badly, especially by children

nursery rhyme (n)
a short rhyme for young children often sung (see Cultural notes)

on leave (exp)
if someone is on leave they don't have to go to work for a period of time

on their trail (exp)
when you are following someone or something (see **trail**)

on the right track (exp)
when you are beginning to understand a situation (see **track**)

(to be) on your guard (exp)
expecting danger and so to be prepared for it

optimistic (adj)
hopeful about the future or about the success of something

overhear (v)
to hear what a person is saying when they are not talking to you and do not know that you are listening

parachute (n)
a device which enables a person to jump from an aircraft and float safely to the ground

Parashot
(see Cultural notes)

patriotism (n)
a strong feeling of love, support and defence of your country

patrol (v)
when guards move around an area to make sure there is no trouble or danger there

persecution (n)
an attack on a person because of their race, belief or religion

pier (n)
a large platform which sticks out into the sea and which people can walk along

pistol (n)
a small handgun

plum (n)
a small sweet fruit with a smooth red or yellow skin and a stone in the middle

porter (n)
a person whose job is to carry things, for example people's luggage at a railway station

proof (n)
a fact or a piece of evidence which shows that something is true or exists

propaganda (n)
information, which is often inaccurate, distributed by an organization in order to influence people

proposal (n)
a suggestion or plan, often formal or written

prowl (v)
to move around quietly, for example when hunting

puddle (n)
a small shallow pool of rain or other liquid on the ground

ransom (n)
money that is demanded as payment for the return of someone who has been kidnapped

reference (n)
a letter written by someone who knows you which describes your character and abilities

refugee (n)
a person who has been forced to leave their country because there is a war there or because of their political or religious beliefs

routine (adj)
activities done regularly as a normal part of a job or process

safe (n)
a strong, metal cupboard with special locks, in which you keep money, jewellery, or other valuable things

safe and sound (exp)
in no danger and in good condition

scapegoat (n)
someone who is blamed or punished for something that is not their fault so that the guilty people escape blame or punishment

shawl (n)
a large piece of woollen cloth worn over a woman's shoulders or head, or wrapped around a baby to keep it warm

shed (n)
a small building used for storing things such as garden tools

shiver (v)
to shake slightly because you are cold or frightened

shoelaces (n)
long, thin pieces of material that are used to fasten your shoes

shortage (n)
when there is not enough of something

sigh (v)
to let out a deep breath, often expressing tiredness or sadness

skid (v)
to move sideways or forwards in an uncontrolled way

smuggler (n)
a person who takes something from one country to another illegally

snore (v)
to make a loud noise each time you breathe while you are asleep

soak (v)
to leave something in a liquid or to wet something completely with a liquid

so-called (adj)
used to describe something that you think is incorrect or not exactly true

spy (v)
to try to find out secret information about other countries or organizations

stare (v)
to look for a long time

sticking plaster (n)
a strip of sticky material with a small pad, used for covering small cuts or sores on your body

stroke (v)
to move your hand slowly and gently over a person, animal or object

suspicion (n)
a belief or feeling that someone has committed a crime or done something wrong

tap (n)
a device that controls the flow of water into a bath or sink

telephone extension (n)
a telephone line, connected to the central switchboard of a company or institution, that has its own number

tension (n)
a feeling of worry and nervousness

threatening (adj)
likely to harm or hurt

thump (n)
a loud noise produced by hitting something hard

track (n)
a narrow road or path

trail (n)
a series of marks or other signs left by someone or something as they move along

traitor (n)
someone who secretly helps the enemy and puts their country in danger

trap (n)
a trick that is intended to catch or deceive someone

transmitter (n)
a piece of equipment used for sending television or radio signals

tremble (v)
to shake slightly, usually because you are frightened or cold

troops (n)
soldiers

tuppence (n)
short form for 'two pennies'

unconsciousness (n)
the state similar to sleep, caused by a shock, accident, or injury

vast (adj)
extremely large

victim (n)
someone who has been hurt or killed by someone or something

volunteer (n)
someone who offers to do a particular task without being forced to do it

voyage (n)
a long journey on a ship

wages (n)
the amount of money that is regularly paid to someone for the work that they do

warden (n)
an official who is responsible for making sure that certain laws are obeyed

widow (n)
a woman whose husband has died

widower (n)
a man whose wife has died

witness (n)
a person who sees an event, crime or accident

woollen (adj)
made of wool – the hair that grows on sheep and some other animals

yard (n)
a unit of length equal to 36 inches or 91.4 centimetres

Collins
English Readers

ALSO IN THE AGATHA CHRISTIE SERIES

The Mysterious Affair at Styles

Recently, there have been some strange things happening at Styles, a large country house in Essex. Evelyn Howard, a loyal friend to the family for years, leaves the house after an argument with Mrs Inglethorp. Mrs Inglethorp then suddenly falls ill and dies. Has she been poisoned? It is up to the famous Belgian detective, Hercule Poirot, to find out what happened.

The Man in the Brown Suit

Pretty, young Anne Beddingfeld comes to London looking for adventure. But adventure finds her when she sees a man fall off an Underground platform and die on the rails. The police think the death was an accident. But who was the man in the brown suit who examined the body before running away? Anne has only one clue, but she is determined to find the mysterious killer. Anne's adventure takes her on a cruise ship all the way to Cape Town and on into Africa…

The Murder of Roger Ackroyd

Roger Ackroyd was a man who knew too much. He knew the woman he loved had poisoned her first husband. He knew someone was blackmailing her – and now she has killed herself. When Roger Ackroyd is found murdered Hercule Poirot is called in to find out who the killer is.

COLLINS ENGLISH READERS

The Murder at the Vicarage

When Colonel Protheroe is found murdered in the vicar's study, it seems that almost everyone in the village of St Mary Mead had a reason to kill him. This is the first case for Agatha Christie's famous female detective, Miss Marple. She needs to use all her powers of observation and deduction to solve the mystery.

Peril at End House

The famous detective Hercule Poirot is on holiday in the south of England when he meets a young woman called Nick Buckley. Nick has had a lot of mysterious 'accidents'. First, her car brakes failed. Then, a large rock just missed her when she was walking, and later, a painting almost fell on her while she was asleep. Finally, Poirot finds a bullet hole in her hat! Nick is in danger and needs Poirot's help. Can he find the guilty person before Nick is harmed?

Why Didn't They Ask Evans?

Bobby Jones is playing golf . . . terribly. As his ball disappears over the edge of a cliff, he hears a cry. The ball is lost, but on the rocks below he finds a dying man. With his final breath the man opens his eyes and says, 'Why didn't they ask Evans?' Bobby and his adventure-seeking friend Lady Frances, set out to solve the mystery of the dying man's last words, but put their own lives in terrible danger . . .

COLLINS ENGLISH READERS

Death in the Clouds

Hercule Poirot is travelling from France to England by plane. During the journey a passenger is murdered. Someone on the flight is guilty of the crime – but who could have a reason to kill an elderly lady? And how is it possible that no one saw it happen?

Appointment with Death

Mrs Boynton, cruel and hated by her family, is found dead while on holiday in the ancient city of Petra in Jordan. Was it just a weak heart and too much sun that killed her, or was she murdered? By chance, the great detective Hercule Poirot is visiting the country. He has 24 hours to solve the case.

The Moving Finger

Lymstock is a small town with many secrets. Recently several people in the town have received unpleasant anonymous letters. When Mrs Symmington dies in mysterious circumstances after receiving a letter, the people of the town no longer know who they can trust. Who is writing the letters? And why? Miss Marple helps solve the mystery.

COLLINS ENGLISH READERS

THE AGATHA CHRISTIE SERIES

The Mysterious Affair at Styles
The Man in the Brown Suit
The Murder of Roger Ackroyd
The Murder at the Vicarage
Peril at End House
Why Didn't They Ask Evans?
Death in the Clouds
Appointment with Death
N or M?
The Moving Finger
Sparkling Cyanide
Crooked House
They Came to Baghdad
They Do It With Mirrors
A Pocket Full of Rye
After the Funeral
Destination Unknown
Hickory Dickory Dock
4.50 From Paddington
Cat Among the Pigeons

Visit **www.collinselt.com/agathachristie** for language activities and teacher's notes based on this story.